Workshop on Human-Computer Question Answering 2016

Held at the 2016 Conference of the North American Chapter of the Association for Computational Linguistics: Human Language Technologies (NAACL HLT 2016)

San Diego, California, USA
16 June 2016

ISBN: 978-1-5108-2529-1

Printed from e-media with permission by:

Curran Associates, Inc.
57 Morehouse Lane
Red Hook, NY 12571

Some format issues inherent in the e-media version may also appear in this print version.

Printed by Curran Associates, Inc. (2016)

For permission requests, please contact the Association for Computational Linguistics at the address below.

Association for Computational Linguistics
209 N. Eighth Street
Stroudsburg, Pennsylvania 18360

Phone: 1-570-476-8006
Fax: 1-570-476-0860

acl@aclweb.org

Additional copies of this publication are available from:

Curran Associates, Inc.
57 Morehouse Lane
Red Hook, NY 12571 USA
Phone: 845-758-0400
Fax: 845-758-2634
Email: curran@proceedings.com
Web: www.proceedings.com

NAACL HLT 2016

The 2016 Conference of the North American Chapter of the Association for Computational Linguistics: Human Language Technologies

Proceedings of the Workshop on Human-Computer Question Answering

June 16, 2016

Preface

Welcome to the first Workshop on Human-Computer Question Answering (HCQA)! Question answering is a central task in natural language processing (NLP). Unlike other NLP tasks, it also is easy for non-experts to understand when question answering systems perform well (or fail). The goal of this workshop is to bring the community together to discuss the state of the art of question answering and interactively compete with top human trivia masters.

This workshop highlights question answering on the real-world task of quiz bowl, a trivia game in which competitors are asked to identify entities such as battles, novels, and scientific terms. In quiz bowl, a moderator reads a paragraph-long question to two teams, and players are permitted to interrupt the moderator (or "buzz in") with a guess if they feel confident. This setting is especially interesting because acquiring more features (clues) comes with an added cost (the other team may buzz in before you). While computerized question answering systems have previously had success against humans, this workshop will be the first to pit different systems against each other and then have that winner face off against a top human team.

Question answering is a task interesting to both academia and industry. This workshop brings people from both sides to discuss recent progress in QA. We will have a presentation from the IBM Watson team talking about their new Watson Discovery Advisor and the challenges of QA in the industrial setting. Peter Clark will talk about new types of question answering problems that he and his team are solving at the Allen Institute for AI. We also have Zhengdong Lu, Jason Weston, and Richard Socher talking about recent neural network approaches to QA.

This year we have nine papers covering a variety of approaches to QA, including neural networks, crowdsourcing, knowledge graph search, and paraphrasing. Besides common QA tasks such as machine comprehension, (open-domain) factoid QA, we are also excited to see new topics on error analysis of QA systems by crowdsourcing and alignment between text description and paintings for art questions.

At the end of the workshop, we will have a dual computer-human tournament to test entrants' question answering systems against each other and against the top human trivia masters. Enjoy the match!

Finally, we invite you to enjoy this volume and we are looking forward to seeing you in San Diego!

Mohit Iyyer, He He, Jordan Boyd-Graber and Hal Daumé III

Organizers:

Mohit Iyyer, University of Maryland, College Park
He He, University of Maryland, College Park
Jordan Boyd-Graber, University of Colorado, Boulder
Hal Daumé III, University of Maryland, College Park

Program Committee:

Mohit Bansal, Toyota Technological Institute at Chicago
Kevin Gimpel, Toyota Technological Institute at Chicago
Edward Grefenstette, Google DeepMind
Sanda Harabagiu, University of Texas at Dallas
Mandar Joshi, University of Washington
Karthik Narasimhan, Massachusetts Institute of Technology
Arvind Neelakantan, University of Massachusetts, Amherst
Mrinmaya Sachan, Carnegie Mellon University
Tomek Strzalkowski, SUNY Albany
Richard Socher, Salesforce
Christina Unger, Bielefeld University
Yi Yang, Georgia Institute of Technology
Wen-Tau Yih, Microsoft Research
Luke Zettlemoyer, University of Washington

Invited Speakers:

Ray Mooney, University of Texas at Austin
Jason Weston, Facebook AI Research
Peter Clark, Allen Institute for AI
Zhengdong Lu, Noah's Ark Lab, Huawei Technologies
Richard Socher, Salesforce
Eunsol Choi, University of Washington

Table of Contents

Conference Program

Thursday, June 16, 2016

9:00–9:15 *Welcome*

Invited Talks I

9:15–9:50 *Invited Talk by Ray Mooney*

9:50–10:25 *Invited Talk by Jason Weston*

10:25–10:40 *Coffee Break*

Talks by Authors of Accepted Papers

10:40-11:00 *Watson Discovery Advisor: Question-answering in an industrial setting*
Charley Beller, Graham Katz, Allen Ginsberg, Chris Phipps, Sean Bethard, Paul Chase, Elinna Shek and Kristen Summers

11:00–11:20 *Crowdsourcing for (almost) Real-time Question Answering*
Denis Savenkov, Scott Weitzner and Eugene Agichtein

11:20–11:40 *Attention-Based Convolutional Neural Network for Machine Comprehension*
Wenpeng Yin, Sebastian Ebert and Hinrich Schütze

11:40–12:00 *Invited Talk by Eunsol Choi*

12:00–1:15 *Lunch*

Invited Talks II

13:15–13:50 ***Invited Talk by Peter Clark***

13:50–14:25 ***Invited Talk by Zhengdong Lu***

14:25–15:00 ***Invited Talk by Richard Socher***

Poster Session

15:00–15:15 ***Coffee Break***

15:15–16:00 *Open-domain Factoid Question Answering via Knowledge Graph Search*
Ahmad Aghaebrahimian

15:15–16:00 *Neural Enquirer: Learning to Query Tables in Natural Language*
Pengcheng Yin, Zhengdong Lu, Hang Li and kao Ben

15:15–16:00 *Neural Generative Question Answering*
Jun Yin, Xin Jiang, Zhengdong Lu, Lifeng Shang, Hang Li and Xiaoming Li

15:15–16:00 *"A Distorted Skull Lies in the Bottom Center..." Identifying Paintings from Text Descriptions*
Anupam Guha, Mohit Iyyer and Jordan Boyd-Graber

15:15–16:00 *Using Confusion Graphs to Understand Classifier Error*
Davis Yoshida and Jordan Boyd-Graber

15:15–16:00 *Paraphrase for Open Question Answering: New Dataset and Methods*
Ying Xu, Pascual Martínez-Gómez, Yusuke Miyao and Randy Goebel

Thursday, June 16, 2016 (continued)

Exhibition Match

16:00–17:15 ***Best Shared Task System vs. Human Quiz Bowl Team***

Watson Discovery Advisor: Question-answering in an industrial setting

Charles Beller and **Graham Katz** and **Allen Ginsberg** and **Chris Phipps**
cebeller@us.ibm.com, egkatz@us.ibm.com, abginsbe@us.ibm.com, phippsc@us.ibm.com

Sean Bethard and **Paul Chase** and **Elinna Shek** and **Kristen Summers**
slbethar@us.ibm.com, pjchase@us.ibm.com, eshek@us.ibm.com, kmsummer@us.ibm.com

IBM Watson Group
Chantilly, VA, United States

Abstract

This work discusses a mix of challenges arising from Watson Discovery Advisor (WDA), an industrial strength descendant of the Watson Jeopardy! Question Answering system currently used in production in industry settings. Typical challenges include generation of appropriate training questions, adaptation to new industry domains, and iterative improvement of the system through manual error analyses.

1 Introduction

Question answering has been a focus for research in computational linguistics and natural language processing since early efforts in the 1960s (Simmons, 1970). Systems such as BASEBALL (Green Jr. et al., 1961) focused on specific, circumscribed domains, e.g. questions about baseball games. As computing power and knowledge resources developed, answering questions over a broad open domain became a focus of engineers and researchers in government, industry, academic settings (Voorhees, 1999; Wang, 2006). Various approaches to question answering have exploited logical forms and logic provers (Moldovan et al., 2003a), relationship matching over structured knowledge bases (Yao and Van Durme, 2014), and the wisdom of the masses via social media analysis (Bian et al., 2008) or crowd-sourcing (Boyd-Graber et al., 2012).

Open-Domain question answering received a wave of renewed attention when IBM's Watson system successfully competed with human champions in the Jeopardy! challenge. That system was developed into the Watson Discovery Advisor IBM product, which we describe below.

2 Watson Discovery Advisor

The Watson Discovery Advisor product (WDA) is a direct descendant of the Watson Jeopardy! system described in (Ferrucci et al., 2010; Ferrucci, 2012). The core processing pipelines are built on the Apache UIMA architecture (Ferrucci and Lally, 2004) and consist of a question-analysis phase (Lally et al., 2012; Kalyanpur et al., 2012), a document and passage retrieval phase, an answer generation phase (Chu-Carroll et al., 2012), an answer scoring phase, and an answer merging and ranking phase (Gondek et al., 2012).

There are several important differences between the Jeopardy! task and the question answering task performed by WDA. At the most superficial level, the Jeopardy! task provides an input consisting of a declarative clue, and expects an interrogative question, i.e. it's an Answer-Questioning task. In reality though, this tends to be a simple syntactic transformation. A more important difference is that Jeopardy! clues are always accompanied by *category* information. In some cases, this category level information is crucial, giving explicit parameters that restrict the range of answers to be considered.

Another difference has to do with the nature of the input questions. Jeopardy! includes a range of puzzle-type questions that required special logic (Prager et al., 2012), these kinds of trick questions do not typically have any place in an industrial question-answering setting. Even without these trick

Proceedings of 2016 NAACL Human-Computer Question Answering Workshop, pages 1–7,
San Diego, California, June 12-17, 2016.

questions, though, Jeopardy! questions do not look like the typical questions that users pose to WDA.

Consider an important element identified as part of question analysis, the *focus* of a question or clue. The focus is the element that, if replaced with a correct answer, will result in a true sentence. In Jeopardy! clues, the focus often contains considerably more information than a formulation of an equivalent question by a user. For example, where a Jeopardy! clue might read *This home of the Eiffel Tower is the capital of France*, a user might simply enter *What is the capital of France?*. Where the simple question can be answered only if a single fact is known, the Jeopardy! style clue provides two independent ways to answer, i.e. knowing the capital of France, or knowing the home of the Eiffel Tower. Such relative impoverishment of user questions as compared to Jeopardy! clues is typical.

3 System Tuning

When WDA is deployed to a new customer, its capabilities are tuned for that customer's particular use case and setting. The first step in tuning is to identify domain appropriate data that will be ingested into the knowledge base. In the case of a financial information discovery application, for example, financial news documents and shareholder reports might be identified. Once appropriate data has been identified and acquired, the main task is to train WDA's answer ranking models. Like the original Jeopardy! system, WDA uses a supervised ranking model that requires a large set of question-answer pairs.

The original Jeopardy! system was trained on past Jeopardy! questions and answers collected from the J! Archive.[1] In industrial applications the QA sets are instead tailored to reflect customer domain interests. Development of these question sets is discussed in Section 3.1. In tandem with developing QA sets, WDA is typically also fed terminology, jargon, and differences in word usage from the domains of interest. This can include significant detailed domain-specific knowledge; e.g., names for corporate entities and financial instruments.

[1] *www.j-archive.com*

3.1 QA Training Data Development

For Watson Discovery Advisor, the bulk of training data is composed of sets of question-answer pairs (QA sets). These QA sets make up the labeled data used to train the system's ranking models. Each QA pair consists of a factoid question with a canonical answer and a set of variant forms for the answer. Variants might include nicknames, acronyms, or alternative spellings. The size of domain-specific QA sets ranges from several hundreds to many thousands. As with many supervised learning scenarios, more is typically better.

As WDA has matured through client engagements, QA sets have been developed for a wide variety of domains, providing a variety of hard-won lessons. The primary goal of Question Answer development is to exercise the feature space sufficiently in model training that WDA's answer ranking models recognize what makes a good factoid answer for a particular domain. The feature space is complex and includes feature scorers that are sensitive to a range of phenomena, from syntactic features of questions, relationships between questions and evidence passages, and orthographic details of answer candidates to connections between terms in evidence passages and internal ontologies or other knowledge resources. To best develop effective models, QA sets must consist of factoid questions with a variety of syntactic structures, based on specific domains and topics, and possessing unambiguous answers.

Ensuring this last condition is not a simple task. Most questions can have a range of possible answers, depending on what kind of information a person is looking for, and even identifying all variant names for a single entity is a challenge. For example, the question *Who won the World Cup?* seems like it should have a simple answer. However, there are several very different and equally plausible answers, depending on what the asker is looking for. Is the question asking about the FIFA world cup or an event from some other sport like cricket, rugby, or chess? Which year's world cup is being asked about? Is the question about the men's or the women's event? Is the question asking for the player who scored the winning goal, or the team?

In our experience, a good factoid question contains disambiguating information within it and has a single, identifiable answer. There are some common mistakes people make when generating factoid questions. We list these below:

- ambiguous questions
- questions missing key references or context
- questions with confusing grammar or wording
- questions with incorrect or incomplete answers
- opinion questions
- non-English questions for an English system
- overly detailed questions
- question irrelevant to the desired domain
- trick questions
- complex question types

These break down into two broad types of (human) errors. At the top of the list are features that make a poor training question because they provide insufficient or insufficiently extractable information for a system to identify a single answer. Towards the bottom of the list are features that make a poor training question because they diverge too greatly from the typical inputs a user would provide. These classes are not mutually exclusive, features in the middle of the list are often combinations of the two.

Specifying answers is also difficult. Even unambiguous factoid questions can have multiple forms of a correct answer. For example, the simple factoid question *Which writer created the TV sitcom '30 Rock'?* has one unambiguous answer, but there are at least five common variants observed in documents: *Tina Fey*, *Elizabeth Stamatina Fey*, *Elizabeth Stamatina "Tina" Fey*, *Ms. Fey*, and *Fey*. Since it is not at all clear which of these should be taken to be the one objectively correct answer, and in general a variety of answers are accepted as correct by users and judges alike, variants must be listed to prevent WDA from learning to avoid generating answers that might well be taken to be correct.

Developing good domain-specific QA sets is one of the major challenges to adapting the WDA system to a new domain. Once QA sets are developed, the system can be trained and evaluated. At this point further progress can be driven by error analysis. The goal is to identify what questions the system still fails on, and more importantly: Why?

3.2 Error Analysis

To tune the system and assess gaps in Watson's knowledge base, the system is evaluated on a held-out test set of QA pairs, which, after processing by the system, is subjected to detailed Error Analysis (Moldovan et al., 2003b; Tellex et al., 2003). Incorrectly answered questions are automatically assigned to several broad error classes, then manually categorized into more detailed sub-classes of error. The automatic deterministic classification of errors is done to bin the errors into the following classes:

- *No Search Hits:* Questions for which the generated search queries fail to retrieve any passage from the corpus that contains the correct answer to the question
- *Unextracted Answers:* Questions for which the retrieved passages contain correct answers, but none of these answers are generated as hypotheses
- *Imperfect Answers:* Questions for which one of the answers generated as a hypothesis partially matches the correct answers
- *Correct Answer 2-10:* Questions for which the correct answer is hypothesized, but ranked below the top answer
- *Correct Answer 11-100:* Questions for which the correct answer is hypothesized, but ranked well below the top answer

These initial bins are the starting point for the programmatic error analysis, as they tend to reflect the likely system component to which the error can be attributed. Broadly speaking the potential loci for error are the following system components:

- the *ingested corpora* might not contain a document that answers the question,
- the *search component* might fail to identify a responsive document passage,
- the *answer generators* might fail to hypothesize the correct or complete answer from a responsive passage,
- the *answer scorers* and *rankers* might fail to rank the correct answer highly.

Once the major error-contributing component is identified, attempts are made to articulate more clearly the exact source of error. For example, answer generation-related errors might arise in a number of different situations, such as incorrect tokenization or problems with anaphora resolution and coreference.

Further Considerations Error analysis for a question-answering system which is deployed to customer application is somewhat more nuanced in its evaluation than standard academic metrics such as accuracy would reveal. While returning a correct answer is important, and returning more correct answers is ideal, there are other considerations. Among these are the topical domains of specialization: In our setting, it is clearly more important to answer correct questions that are of vital importance to a customers core informational needs then it is to correctly answer trivia questions. Of additional importance is that questions which are answered incorrectly are at least answered reasonably. For example, to the question *How many people have been on the moon?* an answer of *Ten* instead of the correct *Twelve* is understandable by a client. It is the kind of error that anyone might make. An answer of *Three pounds* is not. Improving both targeted accuracy (accuracy on a question set relevant to customer concerns) and reasonableness are important goals for industrial applications.

4 Watson on Quiz Bowl

In recent work on Question Answering, data from the Quiz Bowl competitions has played a central role (Boyd-Graber et al., 2015; Iyyer et al., 2014). While the goal of the Watson Discovery Advisor is to address the information discovery concerns of real-world customers, the authors thought there might be some interest in seeing how well WDA played Quiz Bowl. Unfortunately, issues with the answer key make a quantitative evaluation impossible. Despite this, a qualitative evaluation showed some interesting results. In the this section we discuss the issues raised by this attempt.

4.1 WDA plays (limited) Quiz Bowl

A number of History-domain test items from the Iyyer, et al., set were put to an untrained and untuned WDA instance. WDA comes "out of the box" trained on domain general questions not unlike those of Quiz Bowl. We configured the knowledge base to consist primarily of Wikipedia data. While WDA provided answers to the complete data set, automatic evaluation was impossible due to issues with the answer key. On inspection it became clear that many of the answers generated by WDA which did not match the answer key were acceptable variants of the correct answer.[2] For example, the question *For 10 points (FTP), name this antitrust act passed in 1914, which augmented the Sherman antitrust act* was listed as having the answer *Clayton Antitrust Act*. WDA's top ranked answer was *Clayton Act*, which is clearly correct.

To provide an appropriate quantitative assessment of WDA's capabilities, we would need to manually identify all cases of incorrectly answered questions for which returned answer was an acceptable variant of the correct answer. Unfortunately this information is unavailable in the open data set. We do note some interesting differences: WDA returns surnames rather than full names for many historical figures (*Truman* for *Harry S Truman*). WDA prefers to avoid repeating nominals from the question in the answer, returning *Waitangi* for *Treaty of Waitangi*, in response to the query: ... *name this* **treaty** *that formally put New Zealand under British rule and sparked the Maori Wars*. In addition there are numerous derivational, inflectional or orthographic variants that judges would likely deem acceptable, such as *St. Petersburg* for *Saint Petersburg* and *Vandal* for *Vandals*, and many others. Further, WDA finds cases of true alternates such as *Bonus Expeditionary Force* for *Bonus Army*. Finally, there are cases where the answer key is simply incorrect: For the clue *Ruling from 1556 to 1605, he also conquered Afghanistan and Baluchistan. FTP name this 16th century emperor, the greatest of the Mughals*, the answer key provides the incorrect *Shah Jahan*, while WDA finds the correct answer, *Emperor Akbar I*.

These issues make an overall quantitative evaluation of WDA on the Quiz Bowl data a challenge. There are, however, a number of cases in which WDA gets a clearly wrong answer. In the next section we discuss an example that illustrates one of the

[2] Approaches that treat answers as labels in a question classification task (e.g. Iyyer, et al. 2014) avoid this issue. We return to QA as classification in section 4.3

difficulties WDA had with Quiz Bowl data.

4.2 Analyzing a Quiz Bowl Example

For the question below the answer is the *War of 1812*.

> During this war, Andrew Jackson defeated the Creek at the Battle of Horseshoe Bend. Tecumseh died during the Battle of the Thames in this war. The White House was burned by the British Army during this war. Francis Scott Key composed the "Star Spangled Banner" during this conflict. Impressment of U.S. sailors was a major cause of this war. FTP, what 19th-century war between the U.S. and Britain was named for the year it began.

In our experiment with WDA *War of 1812* occurs at rank 7. The answers at rank 1 through 6 include the candidate answers *Baltimore*, *McHenry*, *Siege of Fort Erie*, etc. All of the candidates come from documents that are relevant to the question and most of the passages selected for candidate generation are highly responsive. What is clear, however, is that the (incorrect) candidates are not the "right type of thing" to be an answer to this question, i.e., they are not wars. One reason these non-war candidates are ranked above the correct answer, in this case, has to do with the identification of the question's *Lexical Answer Type* (LAT), the word or phrase in the question that indicates the type of thing that an answer to the question would be an instance of. WDA's ranking models promote answers which are appropriate to the LAT above those that are not. Since WDA fails to find the LAT for this question (*war*), the correct answer is not appropriately ranked.

One general complication with running WDA on Quiz Bowl questions is that they involve multiple sentences. This complicates the LAT identification task. The version of Watson designed for the Jeopardy! challenge assumed that the question clues would be a single sentence or a structured input of a single sentence clue and a short category label. Both the Watson Jeopardy! system and WDA are optimized for that use case. To deal with the Quiz Bowl questions, the question analysis mechanisms, namely the LAT identification models, would need to be retrained to handle multi-sentence input. We are confident that if this were done, questions like the above would be highly likely to be answered correctly by WDA.

To support this contention, we rephrased the initial multi-sentence clue into the single sentence question: *In which 19th-century war between the U.S. and Britain did Andrew Jackson defeat the Creek at the Battle of Horseshoe Bend?* Under this formulation WDA identifies the correct LAT (*war*) and gets the correct answer in 1st place with 52% confidence. The 2nd (and incorrect) answer, *Civil War* (confidence 23%) is notably also of the correct answer type. Answers 3-10 are not wars, but the system's confidence associated with those answers drops sharply from 7% to 1%.

4.3 Quiz Bowl as Classification

One of the factors making practical question answering so challenging is the sparseness of the data. The vast majority of answers required of a working system are unique and — insofar as the training data consists of the QA sets used to tune the ranking (and other) models — unseen in training. For example, in a set of 5045 simulated-user questions used by IBM Watson to train the WDA system, more than 65% of the answers are unique (they were answers to just one question in the data set). The distribution of answer frequencies follows the familiar Zipfian distribution, with many low frequency items and very few high frequency items (Zipf, 1949) — the ratio of questions to (unique) answers is about 1.8:1. While it appears that Quiz Bowl questions in general have a similar ratio of questions to answers, the Quiz Bowl dataset used as the basis for the experiments by Iyyer et al. (2014) does not. In that data set questions with low-frequency answers are removed. Overall for the the 20407 questions there are only 2370 different answers—a question to answer ratio of nearly 9 to 1. This quantitative difference underscores the qualitative differences between the open-domain question answering task that WDA typically addresses and the more coarse-grained question-labeling tasks described in (Iyyer et al., 2014), which in some ways is more of a classification task.

To explore text classification as a method of "question answering" we applied the IBM Bluemix deep-learning based Natural Language Classifier (*www.bluemix.net*) (Ma et al., 2015; Kurata et al.,

	Iyyer et al.	**IBM Bluemix**
History	82.3%	**84.6%**
Literature	78.7%	**90.7%**

Table 1: Classifier accuracy on history and literature questions.

2016) to the data set.[3] We trained two different short-text classifiers with the NLC, one for History-themed questions and one for Literature-themed questions. Each classifier was trained in a supervised manner to label the full-text of the clue (as input) with the answer string (as label). The History training set had 2708 items and 629 labels, the Literature training set had 4064 items and 812 labels. We applied the History-trained classifier to a held-out 455-item test set of History-themed questions and the Literature-trained classifier to a held-out 596-item test set of Literature-themed questions.[4] Table 1 reports the accuracy achieved by these classifiers along with the best results reported in (Iyyer et al., 2014) on the same data sets.

Such classification methods are, of course, limited in the ways that they can address the true question answering task — the task of answering a question with an answer not seen in the training data. As it happens, there were 26 items in the History test data set whose answer did not appear in the training set. The NLC classifier, as expected, failed to label these items correctly, and we suspect that none of the other classifier-based methods did either. We ran this small set of data through WDA, identifying acceptable answer variants by hand. WDA answered 20 of these 26 questions correctly, achieving an accuracy of 76% on this (admittedly small) data set.

5 Discussion

Our test run of WDA on a portion of the Quiz Bowl question set raises some issues with regard to the differences of doing question-answering for real world clients and domains versus domains like Jeopardy! and Quiz Bowl. As discussed in Section 2, one of the key differences is the amount of information, essentially clues or hints, that a question provides. Experience has shown that the average question length in real-world engagements is very short compared to that of Quiz Bowl and Jeopardy! type questions. This has a direct effect on search-query generation for passage retrieval and all subsequent processing. Upon inspection, a small sample of queries generated from Quiz Bowl questions had an average of 69.2 simple query terms.[5] A comparable sample of queries generated from WDA training questions had an average of 8.6 simple query terms, about 1/8th as many.[6] For this reason, search results returned in a real-world system will tend to cover a broader set of topics than in the more constrained search engendered by the Quiz Bowl setting. The richness of the Quiz Bowl clues makes finding relevant documents a much easier task than it is in the world of industrial question answering. One potentially valuable avenue for research involves robustly expanding sparse queries to generate better search results.

6 Conclusion

Using an open domain question answering system in a production setting offers a number of challenges distinct from those encountered in research and game-playing settings. We have discussed techniques and strategies for adapting and improving a Watson Discovery Advisor question answering system to improve performance in any particular production environment. Additionally we provided an outline of our Error Analysis process on cases in which WDA was applied to Quiz Bowl data and demonstrated the effectiveness of the IBM Natural Language Classifier on this data. Furthermore, we were able to show how effectively WDA performed on cases in which classifier-based methods failed.

Acknowledgments

The authors would like to thank Will Dubyak and Dick Darden for their invaluable technical guidance and mentorship, and we thank Brian Keith for his leadership and vision. We also thank Bowen Zhou for the robust Natural Language Classifier service that we used in the Quiz Bowl experiments.

[3]For this method, the issues with the answer key raised above are, with the exception of the actual errors, irrelevant, since the answer key is normalized.

[4]For line-length reasons a small number of test and training items had to be excluded from this experiment.

[5]In this context, simple query terms encompass both atomic terms and alternations (logical OR).

[6]N=5 for both samples. Max: 83 min: 52 for Quiz Bowl, max: 12, min: 7 for WDA

References

Jiang Bian, Yandong Liu, Eugene Agichtein, and Hongyuan Zha. 2008. Finding the right facts in the crowd: factoid question answering over social media. In *Proceedings of the 17th international conference on World Wide Web*, pages 467–476. ACM.

Jordan Boyd-Graber, Brianna Satinoff, He He, and Hal Daumé III. 2012. Besting the quiz master: Crowdsourcing incremental classification games. In *Proceedings of the 2012 Joint Conference on Empirical Methods in Natural Language Processing and Computational Natural Language Learning*, pages 1290–1301. Association for Computational Linguistics.

Jordan Boyd-Graber, Mohit Iyyer, He He, and Hal Daumé III. 2015. Interactive incremental question answering. In *Neural Information Processing Systems*.

Jennifer Chu-Carroll, James Fan, BK Boguraev, David Carmel, Dafna Sheinwald, and Chris Welty. 2012. Finding needles in the haystack: Search and candidate generation. *IBM Journal of Research and Development*, 56(3.4):6–1.

David Ferrucci and Adam Lally. 2004. Uima: an architectural approach to unstructured information processing in the corporate research environment. *Natural Language Engineering*, 10(3-4):327–348.

David Ferrucci, Eric Brown, Jennifer Chu-Carroll, James Fan, David Gondek, Aditya A Kalyanpur, Adam Lally, J William Murdock, Eric Nyberg, John Prager, et al. 2010. Building watson: An overview of the deepqa project. *AI magazine*, 31(3):59–79.

David A Ferrucci. 2012. Introduction to this is watson. *IBM Journal of Research and Development*, 56(3.4):1–15.

DC Gondek, Adam Lally, Aditya Kalyanpur, J William Murdock, Pablo Ariel Duboué, Lei Zhang, Yue Pan, ZM Qiu, and Chris Welty. 2012. A framework for merging and ranking of answers in deepqa. *IBM Journal of Research and Development*, 56(3.4):14–1.

Bert F Green Jr., Alice K Wolf, Carol Chomsky, and Kenneth Laughery. 1961. Baseball: an automatic question-answerer. In *Papers presented at the May 9-11, 1961, Western Joint IRE-AIEE-ACM Computer Conference*, pages 219–224. ACM.

Mohit Iyyer, Jordan Boyd-Graber, Leonardo Claudino, Richard Socher, and Hal Daumé III. 2014. A neural network for factoid question answering over paragraphs. In *Empirical Methods in Natural Language Processing*.

Aditya Kalyanpur, Siddharth Patwardhan, BK Boguraev, Adam Lally, and Jennifer Chu-Carroll. 2012. Fact-based question decomposition in DeepQA. *IBM Journal of Research and Development*, 56(3.4):13–1.

Gakuto Kurata, Bing Xiang, and Bowen Zhou. 2016. Improved neural network-based multi-label classification with better initialization leveraging label co-occurrence. In *Proceedings of NAACL/HLT 2016*.

Adam Lally, John M Prager, Michael C McCord, BK Boguraev, Siddharth Patwardhan, James Fan, Paul Fodor, and Jennifer Chu-Carroll. 2012. Question analysis: How watson reads a clue. *IBM Journal of Research and Development*, 56(3.4):2–1.

Mingbo Ma, Liang Huang, Bing Xiang, and Bowen Zhou. 2015. Dependency-based convolutional neural networks for sentence embedding. *Volume 2: Short Papers*, page 174.

Dan Moldovan, Christine Clark, Sanda Harabagiu, and Steve Maiorano. 2003a. Cogex: A logic prover for question answering. In *Proceedings of the 2003 Conference of the North American Chapter of the Association for Computational Linguistics on Human Language Technology-Volume 1*, pages 87–93. Association for Computational Linguistics.

Dan Moldovan, Marius Paşca, Sanda Harabagiu, and Mihai Surdeanu. 2003b. Performance issues and error analysis in an open-domain question answering system. *ACM Transactions on Information Systems (TOIS)*, 21(2):133–154.

John M Prager, Eric W Brown, and Jennifer Chu-Carroll. 2012. Special questions and techniques. *IBM Journal of Research and Development*, 56(3.4):11–1.

Robert F Simmons. 1970. Natural language question-answering systems: 1969. *Communications of the ACM*, 13(1):15–30.

Stefanie Tellex, Boris Katz, Jimmy Lin, Aaron Fernandes, and Gregory Marton. 2003. Quantitative evaluation of passage retrieval algorithms for question answering. In *Proceedings of the 26th annual international ACM SIGIR conference on Research and development in informaion retrieval*, pages 41–47. ACM.

Ellen M Voorhees. 1999. The trec-8 question answering track report. In *Proceedings of the 8th Text REtrieval Conference (TREC-8)*, pages 77–82.

Mengqiu Wang. 2006. A survey of answer extraction techniques in factoid question answering. *Computational Linguistics*, 1(1).

Xuchen Yao and Benjamin Van Durme. 2014. Information extraction over structured data: Question answering with freebase. In *ACL (1)*, pages 956–966. Citeseer.

George Kingsley Zipf. 1949. *Human behavior and the principle of least effort*. Addison-Wesley Press.

Crowdsourcing for (almost) Real-time Question Answering

Denis Savenkov
Emory University
dsavenk@emory.edu

Scott Weitzner
Emory University
sweitzn@emory.edu

Eugene Agichtein
Emory University
eugene@mathcs.emory.edu

Abstract

Modern search engines have made dramatic progress in the answering of many user's questions about facts, such as those that might be retrieved or directly inferred from a knowledge base. However, many other questions that real users ask are more complex, such as asking for opinions or advice for a particular situation, and are still largely beyond the competence of the computer systems. As conversational agents become more popular, QA systems are increasingly expected to handle such complex questions, and to do so in (nearly) real-time, as the searcher is unlikely to wait longer than a minute or two for an answer. One way to overcome some of the challenges in complex question answering is crowdsourcing. We explore two ways crowdsourcing can assist a question answering system that operates in (near) real time: by providing answer validation, which could be used to filter or re-rank the candidate answers, and by creating the answer candidates directly. Specifically, we focus on understanding the effects of time restrictions in the near real-time QA setting. Our experiments show that even within a one minute time limit, crowd workers can produce reliable ratings for up to three answer candidates, and generate answers that are better than an average automated system from the LiveQA 2015 shared task. Our findings can be useful for developing hybrid human-computer systems for automatic question answering and conversational agents.

1 Introduction

It has long been a dream to communicate with a computer as one might with another human being using natural language speech and text. Nowadays, we are coming closer to this dream, as natural language interfaces become increasingly popular. Our phones are already reasonably good at recognizing speech, and personal assistants, such as Apple Siri, Google Now, Microsoft Cortana, Amazon Alexa, etc., help us with everyday tasks and answer some of our questions. Chat bots are arguably considered "the next big thing", and a number of startups developing this kind of technology has emerged in Silicon Valley and around the world[1].

Question answering is one of the major components of such personal assistants. Existing techniques already allow users to get direct answers to their factoid questions. However, there is still a large number of more complex questions, such as advice or accepted general opinions, for which users have to dig into the "10 blue links" and extract or synthesize answers from information buried within the retrieved documents. To cater to these informational needs, community question answering (CQA) sites emerged, such as Yahoo! Answers and Stack Exchange. These sites provide a popular way to connect information seekers with answerers. Unfortunately, it can take minutes or hours, and sometimes days, for the community to respond, and some questions are left unanswered altogether.

To facilitate research on this challenge, TREC

[1]http://time.com/4194063/chatbots-facebook-messenger-kik-wechat/

Proceedings of 2016 NAACL Human-Computer Question Answering Workshop, pages 8–14,
San Diego, California, June 12-17, 2016.

LiveQA shared task[2] was started in 2015, where automated systems attempt to answer real users' questions within a 1 minute period. This task was successful, with the winning system able to automatically return a reasonable answer to more than half of the submitted questions, as assessed for TREC by the trained judges from NIST. Nevertheless, many questions were unable to be answered well by any of the participating systems.

In this work we explore two ways common crowdsourcing can be used to help an automated system answer complex user questions in near real-time scenario, e.g., within a minute. More specifically, we study if crowd workers can quickly and reliably judge the quality of the proposed answer candidates, and if it is possible to obtain reasonable written answers from the crowd within a limited amount of time. Our research questions can be stated as:

1. RQ1. Can crowdsourcing be used to judge the quality of answers to non-factoid questions under a time limit?
2. RQ2. Is it possible to use crowdsourcing to collect answers to real user questions under a time limit?
3. RQ3. How does the quality of crowdsourced answers to non-factoid questions compare to original CQA answers, and to automatic answers from TREC LiveQA systems?

2 Methodology

To answer the research questions, we conducted a series of crowdsourcing experiments using the Amazon Mechanical Turk platform[3]. We used questions from the TREC LiveQA 2015 shared task, along with the system answers, rated by the NIST assessors[4]. The questions for the task were selected by the organizers from the live stream of questions posted to the Yahoo! Answers CQA platform on the day of the challenge (August 31, 2015). For these questions we also crawled their community answers, that were eventually posted on Yahoo! Answers[5].

To check if crowdsourcing can be used to judge the quality of answers under a time limit (RQ1), we asked workers to rate answers to a sample of 100 questions using the official TREC rating scale:

1. Bad - contains no useful information
2. Fair - marginally useful information
3. Good - partially answers the question
4. Excellent - fully answers the question

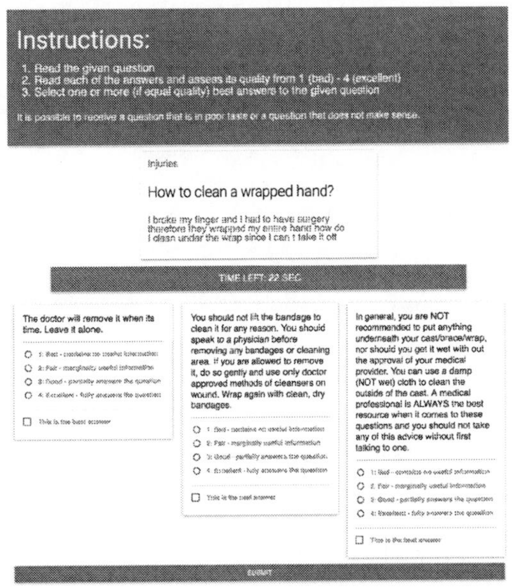

Figure 1: Answer validation form

We chose to display 3 answers for a question, which were generated by three of the top-10 automatic systems from TREC LiveQA 2015 evaluation (Agichtein et al., 2015). To study the effect of time pressure on the quality of judgments we split participants into two groups. One group made their assessments with a 1 minute countdown timer shown to them, while the other could complete the task without worrying about a time limit. Within each group, we assigned three different workers per question, and the workers were compensated at a rate of $0.05 per question for this task.

The interface for collecting answer ratings is illustrated in Figure 1[6]. On top of the interface workers were shown the instructions on the task, and question and answers were hidden at this time. They

[2] www.trec-liveqa.org

[3] http://mturk.com

[4] https://sites.google.com/site/trecliveqa2016/liveqa-qrels-2015

[5] As the answer we took the top question, which was selected as the "Best answer" by the author of the question or by the community.

[6] The screenshots show the final state of the form, as we describe later in this sections fields were unhidden step-by-step for proper timing of reading, answering and validation

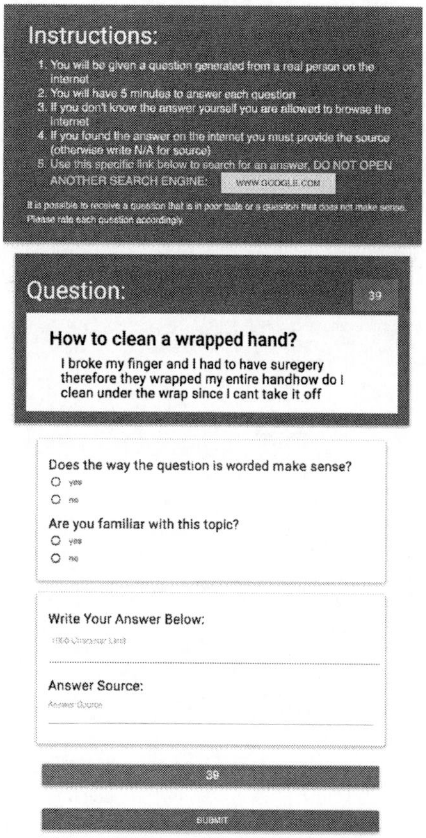

Figure 2: Answer crowdsourcing form

were instructed to read the question, read the answers, and rate each answer's quality on a scale from 1 (Bad) to 4 (Excellent), and finally choose a subset of candidates that best answer the question. Upon clicking a button to indicate that they were done reading the instructions, the question, a 60 second countdown timer and 3 answers to the question appeared on the screen. At the 15 second mark the timer color changed from green to red. In the experiments without time pressure the timer was hidden, but we still tracked the time it took for the workers to complete the task.

In another experiment, designed to answer RQ2 and check whether crowd workers can provide an answer to a given question within a limited amount of time, we asked different workers to answer the questions from TREC LiveQA 2015. We split the workers into two groups and displayed a one minute countdown timer for one of them. We left a grace period and let the workers submit their answers after the timer had run out. The workers received a $0.10 compensation for each answer. The form for answer crowdsourcing is shown in Figure 2, and similar to the answer rating form, it starts with a set of instructions for the task. We let the users browse the internet if they were not familiar with the topic or could not answer the question themselves. To prevent them from finding the original question on Yahoo! Answers, we included a link to Google search engine with a date filter enabled[7]. Using this link, workers could search the web as it was on 8/30/2015, before TREC LiveQA 2015 questions were posted and therefore workers were in the same conditions as automatic systems on the day of challenge[8]. Initially, the question was hidden for proper accounting of question-reading and answering times. Upon clicking a button to indicate that they were done reading the instructions, a question appeared along with a button, which needed to be clicked to indicate that they were done reading the question. After that, the answering form appears, it contained four fields:

1. Does the question make sense: "yes" or "no" to see if the question was comprehensible
2. Are you familiar with the topic: A yes or no question to evaluate whether the worker has had prior knowledge regarding the question topic
3. Answer: the field to be used for the user's answer to the given question
4. Source: the source used to find the answer: URL of a webpage or NA if the worker used his own expertise

Finally, to compare the quality of the collected answers with automatic system and CQA responses (RQ3) we pooled together the crowdsourced answers, the answers from the winning and other top-10 LiveQA'15 systems, and the original answers crawled from Yahoo! Answers. Each set of answers was given to mechanical turk workers for ratings.

3 Results and Discussion

In this section we will describe our results and discuss some of the implications. We start from the results on answer rating (Section 3.1), and then describe the answer crowdsourcing experiment (Section 3.2).

[7]https://www.google.com/webhp?tbs=cdr:1,cd_max:8/30/2015

[8]The ranking of search results could be different on the day of the challenge and for our workers

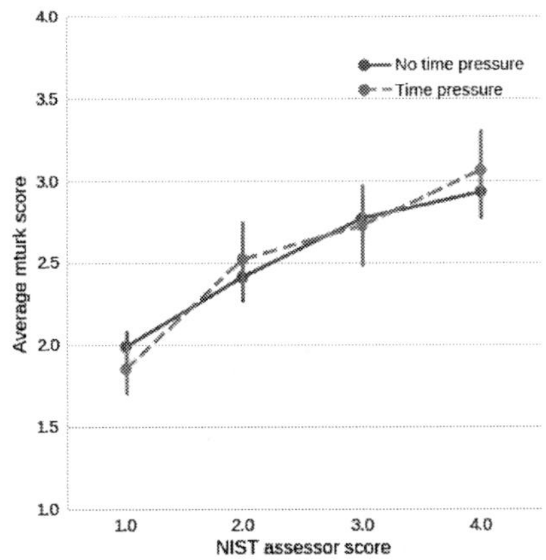

Figure 3: Correlation between NIST assessor scores and crowdsourced ratings with and without time limit on the work time

3.1 Answer rating

In the answer rating experiment we collected 6 ratings (3 with and 3 without time pressure) for each of three answers for a sample of 100 questions, which makes it a total of 1800 judgments. Each answer also has an official NIST assessor rating on the same scale. Figure 3 shows correlation between official NIST assessor relevance judgments and ratings provided by our workers. The Pearson correlation between the scores is $\rho = 0.52$. The distribution of scores shows that official assessors were very strict and assigned many extreme scores of 1 or 4, whereas mechanical turk workers preferred intermediate 2s and 3s. The results did not show any significant differences between experiments with and without time pressure. Figure 4 shows that even though the median time to rate all three answers is around 22-25 seconds in both experiments, the upper bound is significantly lower in the experiment with the time pressure.

Therefore, we conclude that in general we can trust crowdsourced ratings, and on average one minute is enough to judge the quality of three answers to CQA questions.

3.2 Answer crowdsourcing

In the answer crowdsourcing experiment we collected 6 answers (3 with and without time pressure) for each of the 1087 LiveQA'15 questions. Since we have answers from different sources, let's introduce

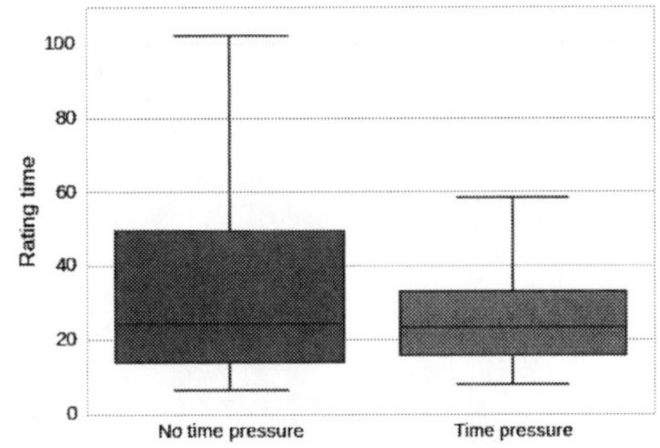

Figure 4: Box plot of answer rating time with and without time pressure

the following notations:

- *Yahoo! Answers* - answers eventually posted by users on Yahoo! Answers for the original questions
- *Crowd* - answers collected from Mechanical Turk workers without time pressure
- *Crowd-time* - answers collected from Mechanical Turk workers with one minute time pressure
- *LiveQA winner* - answers from the TREC LiveQA'15 winning system
- *LiveQA top10* - answers from another top 10 TREC LiveQA'15 system.

Table 1 summarizes some statistics on the answers. The first thing to notice is that, unlike CQA websites, where some questions are left unanswered, by paying the crowd workers we were able to get at least one answer for all LiveQA questions (after filtering "No answer" and "I don't know" kind of responses). The length of the answers, provided by Mechanical turk users is lower, and time pressure forces users to be even more concise. The majority of workers ($\sim 90\%$) didn't use the web search and provided answers based on their experience, opinions and common knowledge.

From Figure 5 we can see that adding time pressure shifts the distribution of answering times[9]. The tail of longer work times for no time limit experiment becomes thin with time restrictions and the distribution peaks around one minute.

To estimate the quality of answers, we took a sample of 100 questions and repeated the answer rating

[9]We had separate timers for reading the instructions, the question, and writing the answer, the inclusion of instruction-reading time is why the total time could be more than 1 minute

Table 1: Statistics of different types of answers for Yahoo! Answers questions

Statistic	Y!A	mTurk	mTurk-time	LiveQA'15 winning system
% answered	78.7%	100.0%	100.0%	97.8%
Length (chars)	354.96	190.83	126.65	790.41
Length (words)	64.54	34.16	22.82	137.23

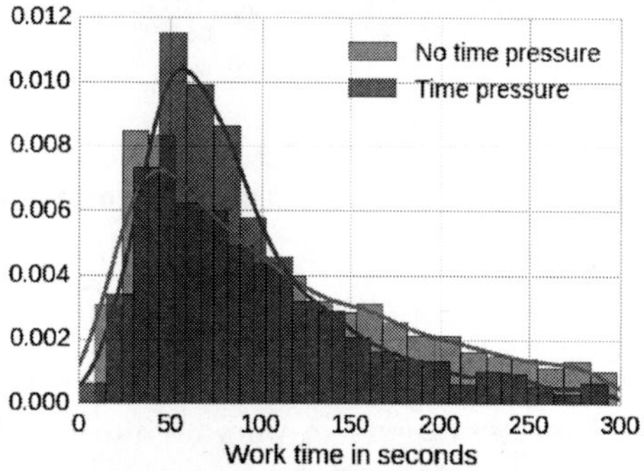

Figure 5: Distribution of answering times for experiments with and without time pressure

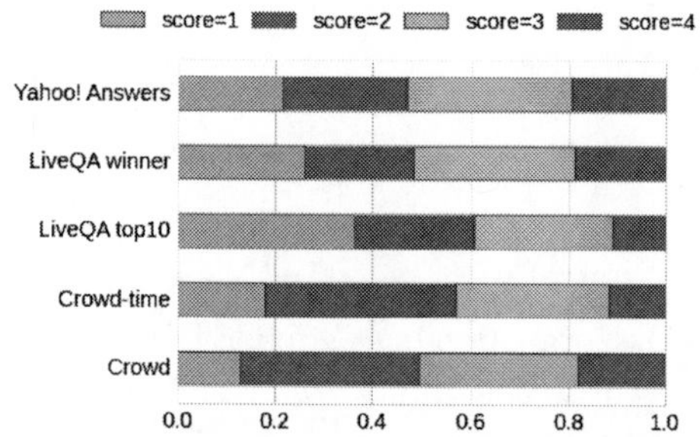

Figure 7: Distribution of scores for different types of answers to Yahoo! Answers questions

experiment on this data. Each answer was judged by 3 different workers (without time pressure), and their scores were averaged. Figure 6 displays the plot with average score for answers from different sources. Quite surprisingly the quality of collected answers turned out be comparable to those of CQA website users. Average rating of answers produced by the winning TREC LiveQA system is also pretty close to human answers. Finally, as expected, time pressure had its negative effect on the quality, however it is still significantly better than quality of an average top 10 QA system.

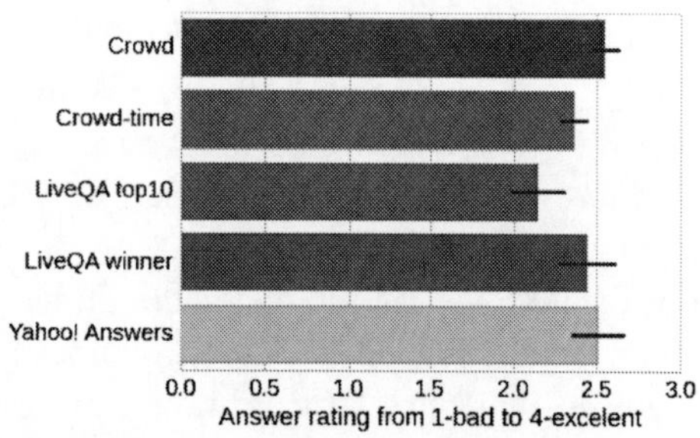

Figure 6: Average scores of different types of answers to Yahoo! Answers questions

Analysis of the score distribution (Figure 7) sheds some light on the nature of the problems with automatic and human answers. The automatic systems generate non-relevant answers ($score = 1$) more often than human, either because the systems fail to retrieve relevant information, or to distinguish between useful and non-useful answer candidates. However, by having a larger information store, e.g., the Web, automated QA systems can often find a perfect answer ($score = 4$), while crowd workers tend to give generally useful, but less perfect responses ($score = 2, 3$).

Our results suggest that the "crowd" can quickly give a reasonable answer to most CQA questions. However, some questions require a certain expertise, which a common crowd worker might not possess. One idea to tackle this challenge is to design a QA information support system, which a worker can use to help them find additional information. For example, in our experiment, we let workers use web search to find answers, if they were unfamiliar with the topic; more effective search interfaces may be helpful.

Overall, the results of our study are encouraging, but there are a number of questions, that need to be addressed in order to build an efficient real-time human-computer QA system, which we leave to future work. For example, in order for a hybrid crowd-automatic QA system to scale to a large number user questions, an efficient crowd gathering and job assignment components are required(Bernstein et al., 2011). One potential approach to scalability is selective crowdsourcing, i.e., that a system consult the crowd only if it does not believe it has a good candidate, or cannot decide between multiple good answers based on internal quality scores. Another promising direction is for a QA system to use the crowd data as a feedback loop, and improve its performance over time, e.g., to update the answer selection and ranking models.

4 Related Work

Using the wisdom of a crowd to help users satisfy their information needs has been studied before in the literature. Bernstein et al. (2012) explored the use of crowdsourcing for offline preparation of answers to tail search queries. In this work log mining techniques were used to identify potential question-answer fragment pairs, which were then processed by the crowd to generate the final answer. This offline procedure allows a search engine to increase the coverage of direct answers to user questions. In our work, however, the focus is on online question answering, which requires fast responses to the user, who is unlikely to wait more than a minute. Another related work is targeting a different domain, namely SQL queries. The CrowdDB system (Franklin et al., 2011) is an SQL-like processing system for queries, that cannot be answered by machines only. In CrowdDB human input is used to collect missing data, perform computationally difficult functions or matching against the query. In Aydin et al. (2014) authors explored efficient ways to combine human input for multiple choice questions from the "Who wants to be a millionaire?" TV show. In this scenario going with the majority for complex questions isn't effective, and certain answerer confidence weighting schemas can improve the results.

Using crowdsourcing for relevance judgments has been studied extensively in the information retrieval community, e.g., (Alonso et al., 2008; Alonso and Baeza-Yates, 2011; Grady and Lease, 2010) to name a few. The focus in these works is on document relevance, and the quality of crowdsourced judgments. Whereas in our paper we are investigating the ability of a crowd to quickly assess the quality of the answers in a nearly real-time setting.

Crowdsourcing is usually associated with offline data collection, which requires significant amount of time. Its application to (near) real-time scenarios poses certain additional challenges. Bernstein et al. (2011) introduced the retainer model for recruiting synchronous crowds for interactive real-time tasks and showed their effectiveness on the best single image and creative generation tasks. We are planning to build on these ideas and integrate a crowd into a real-time question answering system. The work of Lasecki et al. (2013) showed how multiple workers can sit behind a conversational agent named Chorus, where human input is used to propose and vote on responses. Another use of a crowd for maintaining a dialog is presented in Bessho et al. (2012), who let the crowd handle difficult cases, when a system was not able to automatically retrieve a good response from the database of twitter data. In this paper, we focus on a single part of the human-computer dialog, i.e. question answering, which requires a system to provide some useful information in a response to the user.

5 Conclusions

We explored the potential usefulness of crowdsourcing for near real-time question answering, by either directly collecting answers from the crowd, or by using crowdsourced judgments to quickly validate automated answers. Our initial results show that crowd workers are capable of validating a small set of answer candidates quickly, which could be potentially incorporated into an automatic QA system for answer validation and reranking (RQ1). In addition, even one minute appears enough for a crowd to generate a fair or good response to most real questions drawn from a CQA site, which can be useful in case a QA system didn't have good candidates in the first place (RQ2). Finally, we compared crowdsourced answers to the original Yahoo! Answers responses, and to the responses of purely automated LiveQA'15 systems (RQ3). The quality of crowdsourced answers was comparable to the original Yahoo! Answers responses, and even with time pressure, crowdsourcing was shown promising to complement or augment automated QA systems.

ACKNOWLEDGMENTS: This work was partially supported by the Yahoo Labs Faculty Research Engagement Program (FREP).

References

Eugene Agichtein, David Carmel, Donna Harman, Dan Pelleg, and Yuval Pinter. 2015. Overview of the trec 2015 liveqa track. In *Proceedings of TREC 2015*.

Omar Alonso and Ricardo Baeza-Yates. 2011. Design and implementation of relevance assessments using crowdsourcing. In *Advances in information retrieval*, pages 153–164. Springer.

Omar Alonso, Daniel E. Rose, and Benjamin Stewart. 2008. Crowdsourcing for relevance evaluation. *SIGIR Forum*, 42(2):9–15, November.

Bahadir Ismail Aydin, Yavuz Selim Yilmaz, Yaliang Li, Qi Li, Jing Gao, and Murat Demirbas. 2014. Crowdsourcing for multiple-choice question answering. In *AAAI*, pages 2946–2953.

Michael S Bernstein, Joel Brandt, Robert C Miller, and David R Karger. 2011. Crowds in two seconds: Enabling realtime crowd-powered interfaces. In *Proceedings of the 24th annual ACM symposium on User interface software and technology*, pages 33–42. ACM.

Michael S Bernstein, Jaime Teevan, Susan Dumais, Daniel Liebling, and Eric Horvitz. 2012. Direct answers for search queries in the long tail. In *Proceedings of the SIGCHI conference on human factors in computing systems*, pages 237–246. ACM.

Fumihiro Bessho, Tatsuya Harada, and Yasuo Kuniyoshi. 2012. Dialog system using real-time crowdsourcing and twitter large-scale corpus. In *Proceedings of the 13th Annual Meeting of the Special Interest Group on Discourse and Dialogue*, SIGDIAL '12, pages 227–231, Stroudsburg, PA, USA. Association for Computational Linguistics.

Michael J Franklin, Donald Kossmann, Tim Kraska, Sukriti Ramesh, and Reynold Xin. 2011. Crowddb: answering queries with crowdsourcing. In *Proceedings of the 2011 ACM SIGMOD International Conference on Management of data*, pages 61–72. ACM.

Catherine Grady and Matthew Lease. 2010. Crowdsourcing document relevance assessment with mechanical turk. In *Proceedings of the NAACL HLT 2010 workshop on creating speech and language data with Amazon's mechanical turk*, pages 172–179. Association for Computational Linguistics.

Walter S. Lasecki, Rachel Wesley, Jeffrey Nichols, Anand Kulkarni, James F. Allen, and Jeffrey P. Bigham. 2013. Chorus: A crowd-powered conversational assistant. In *Proceedings of the 26th Annual ACM Symposium on User Interface Software and Technology*, UIST '13, pages 151–162, New York, NY, USA. ACM.

Attention-Based Convolutional Neural Network for Machine Comprehension

Wenpeng Yin, Sebastian Ebert, Hinrich Schütze
LMU Munich, Germany
wenpeng, ebert@cis.lmu.de

Abstract

Understanding open-domain text is one of the primary challenges in NLP. Machine comprehension benchmarks evaluate a system's ability to understand text based on the text content only. In this work, we investigate machine comprehension on MCTest, a question answering (QA) benchmark. Prior work is mainly based on feature engineering approaches. We come up with a neural network framework, named hierarchical attention-based convolutional neural network (HABCNN), to address this task without any manually designed features. Specifically, we explore HABCNN for this task by two routes, one is through traditional joint modeling of document, question and answer, one is through textual entailment. HABCNN employs an attention mechanism to detect key phrases, key sentences and key snippets that are relevant to answering the question. Experiments show that HABCNN outperforms prior deep learning approaches by a big margin.

1 Introduction

Machine comprehension is an open-domain question-answering problem which contains factoid questions, but the answers can be derived by extraction or induction of key clues. Figure 1 shows one example in MCTest (Richardson et al., 2013). Each example consists of one document, four associated questions; each question is followed by four answer candidates of which only one is correct. Questions in MCTest have two categories; "one" questions can be answered based on a single sentence from document where "multiple" questions require several sentences. To correctly answer the first question in the example, the two blue sentences are required; for the second question instead, we only need the red sentence. The following observations hold for the whole MCTest. (i) Most of the sentences in the document are irrelevant for a given question. It hints that we need to pay attention to just some key regions. (ii) Answer candidates vary in length and abstraction level and usually do not appear in the document. For example, candidate B for the second question is "outside", which is one word and does not exist in the document, while the answer candidates for the first question are longer texts with some auxiliary words like "Because" in the text. This requires our system to handle flexible texts via *extraction* as well as *abstraction*. (iii) Some questions require multiple sentences to infer the answer, and those vital sentences mostly appear close to each other (we call them *snippet*). Hence, our system should be able to make a choice or compromise between potential single-sentence clue

The road to Grandpa's house was long and winding. [...] Jimmy liked to collect insects on the way to his Grandpa's house, so had picked the longer path. As he went along, Jimmy found more and more insects to add to his jar. [...]. Finally, Jimmy arrived at Grandpa's house and knocked. Grandpa answered the door with a smile and welcomed Jimmy inside. They sat by the fire and talked about the insects. They watched the lightning bugs light up as night came.

1: multiple: Why did Grandpa answer the door?
A) Because he saw the insects
B) Because Jimmy was walking
*C) Because Jimmy knocked
D) Because the trip took a long time

2: one: Where do Jimmy and his Grandpa sit?
A) On insects
B) Outside
*C) By the fire
D) On the path

Figure 1: One example with 2 out of 4 questions in the MCTest. "*" marks correct answer.

Proceedings of 2016 NAACL Human-Computer Question Answering Workshop, pages 15–21,
San Diego, California, June 12-17, 2016.

and snippet clue.

Prior work is mostly based on feature engineering. We take the lead in presenting a deep neural network without linguistic feature engineering.

Concretely, we propose HABCNN, a hierarchical attention-based convolutional neural network, to address this task in two roadmaps. In the first one, we project the document in two different ways, one based on question-attention, one based on answer-attention and then compare the two projected document representations to determine whether the answer matches the question. In the second one, every question-answer pair is reformatted into a statement, then the whole task reduces to textual entailment.

In both roadmaps, convolutional neural network (CNN) is explored to model all types of text. As human beings usually do for such a QA task, our model is expected to be able to detect the key snippets, key sentences, and key words or phrases in the document. In order to detect those informative parts required by questions, we explore an attention mechanism to model the document so that in its representation the required information is emphasized. In practice, instead of imitating human beings in QA task top-down, our system models the document bottom-up, through accumulating the most relevant information from word level to snippet level.

Our approach is novel in three aspects. (i) A document is modeled by a hierarchical CNN for different granularity, from word to sentence level, then from sentence to snippet level. (ii) In the example in Figure 1, apparently not all sentences are required given a question, and usually different snippets are required by different questions. Hence, the same document should have different representations based on what the question is. To this end, attention is incorporated into the hierarchical CNN to guide the learning of dynamic document representations which closely match the information requirements by questions. (iii) Document representations at sentence and snippet levels both are informative for the question. Therefore a highway network is developed to combine them, enabling our system to make a flexible tradeoff.

Overall, we make three contributions. (i) We present a hierarchical attention-based CNN system "HABCNN". It is, to our knowledge, the first deep learning (DL) based system for this MCTest task.

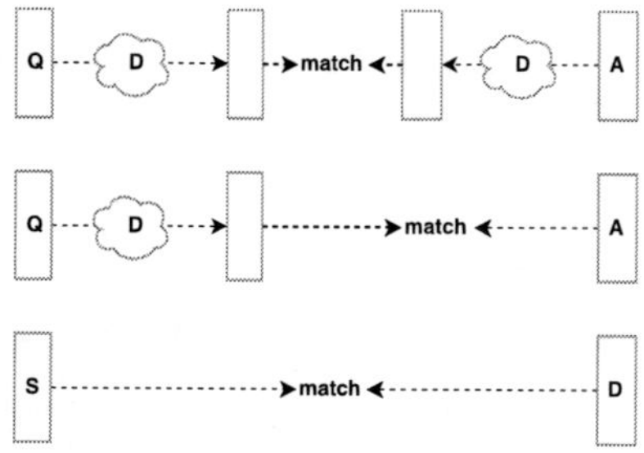

Figure 2: Illustrations of HABCNN-QAP (top), HABCHH-QP (middle) and HABCNN-TE (bottom). Q, A, S: question, answer, statement; D: document

(ii) Prior document modeling systems based on deep neural networks mostly generate generic representation, this work is the first to incorporate attention so that document representation is biased towards the question requirement. (iii) Our HABCNN systems outperform other DL competitors by big margins.

2 Related Work

Existing systems for MCTest are mostly based on manually engineered features, e.g., (Narasimhan and Barzilay, 2015; Sachan et al., 2015; Wang et al., 2015; Smith et al., 2015). In these works, a common route is first to define a loss function based on feature vectors, then the effort focuses on designing effective features based on various rules. Even though this research is groundbreaking for this task, its flexibility and capacity for generalization is limited.

DL approaches appeal to increasing interest in analogous tasks. Weston et al., (2015b) introduce memory networks for factoid QA. Memory network framework is extended in (Weston et al., 2015a; Kumar et al., 2016) for Facebook bAbI dataset. Peng et al. (2015)'s Neural Reasoner infers over multiple supporting facts to generate an entity answer for a given question and it is also tested on bAbI. All of this work deals with short texts with simple grammar, aiming to *generate* an answer that is restricted to be one word denoting a location, a person etc.

There is also work on other kinds of QA, e.g., (Iyyer et al., 2014; Hermann et al., 2015). Overall, for open-domain MCTest machine comprehension task, we are the first to use deep neural networks.

HABCNN shares similarities with the model published by Trischler et al. (2016) six weeks after our submission on arxiv. It considers multiple levels of granularity in a way that is similar to our approach.

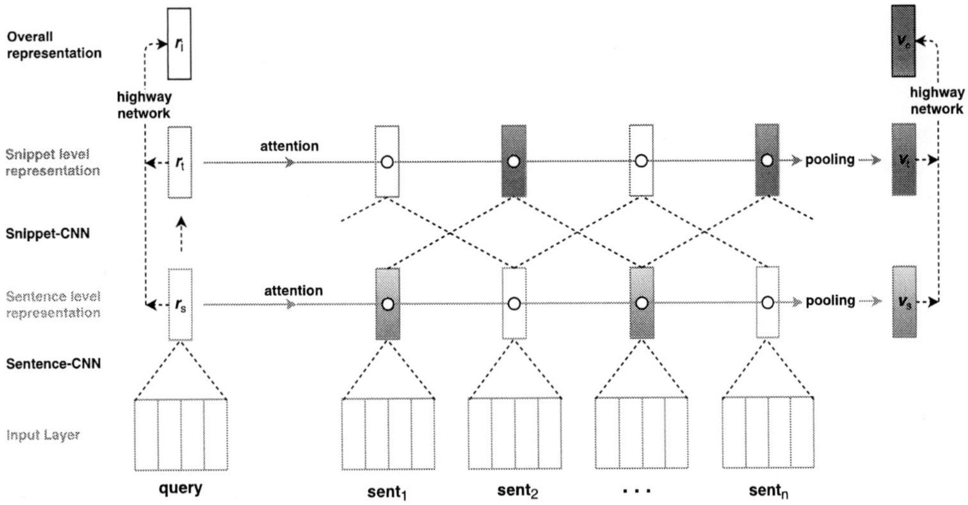

Figure 3: HABCNN. Feature maps for phrase representations $\mathbf{p}_i$ and the max pooling steps that create sentence representations out of phrase representations are omitted for simplification. Each snippet covers three sentences in snippet-CNN. Symbols ∘ mean cosine similarity calculation.

Trischler et al. (2016) achieve better performance than HABCNN, but they still use linguistically engineered features like Stanford dependencies whereas our approach is more truly end-to-end.

3 Model

We investigate this task by three approaches, illustrated in Figure 2. (i) We can compute two different document (D) representations in a common space, one based on question (Q) attention, one based on answer (A) attention, and compare them. This architecture is named HABCNN-QAP ("QAP" means projecting D based on Q and A). (ii) We compute a representation of D based on Q attention (as before), but now we compare it directly with a representation of A. We name this architecture HABCNN-QP. (iii) We treat this QA task as textual entailment (TE), first reformatting Q-A pair into a statement (S), then matching S and D directly. This architecture we name HABCNN-TE. All three approaches are implemented in the common framework HABCNN.

3.1 HABCNN

Recall that we use the abbreviations A (answer), Q (question), S (statement), D (document). HABCNN performs representation learning for triple (Q, A, D) in HABCNN-QP and HABCNN-QAP, for tuple (S, D) in HABCNN-TE. For convenience, we use "query" to refer to Q, A, or S uniformly. HABCNN, depicted in Figure 3, has the following phases.

Input Layer. The input is (query, D). Query is two individual sentences (for Q, A) or one single sentence (for S), D is a sequence of sentences. Words are initialized by d-dimensional pre-trained word embeddings. As a result, each sentence is represented as a feature map with dimensionality of $d \times s$ (s is sentence length). In Figure 3, each sentence in the input layer is depicted by a rectangle with multiple columns.

Sentence-CNN is used for sentence representation learning from word level. Given a sentence of length s with a word sequence: $v_1, v_2, \ldots, v_s$, let vector $\mathbf{c}_i \in \mathbb{R}^{wd}$ be the concatenated embeddings of w words $v_{i-w+1}, \ldots, v_i$ where w is the filter width, d is the dimensionality of word representations and $0 < i < s+w$. Embeddings for words v_i, $i < 1$ and $i > s$, are zero padding. We then generate the representation $\mathbf{p}_i \in \mathbb{R}^{d_1}$ for the *phrase* $v_{i-w+1}, \ldots, v_i$ using the convolution weights $\mathbf{W} \in \mathbb{R}^{d_1 \times wd}$:

$$\mathbf{p}_i = \tanh(\mathbf{W} \cdot \mathbf{c}_i + \mathbf{b}) \quad (1)$$

where bias $\mathbf{b} \in \mathbb{R}^{d_1}$. CNN has $d_1 = s + w - 1$ kernels. Sentence-CNNs for query and all document sentences share the same weights, so that the generated representations are comparable.

Sentence-Level Representation. The sentence-CNN generates a new feature map (omitted in Figure 3) for each input sentence, one column in the feature map denotes a phrase representation (i.e., $\mathbf{p}_i$ in Equation (1)).

For the query and each sentence of D, we do *element-wise 1-max-pooling* ("max-pooling" for short) (Collobert and Weston, 2008) over phrase representations to form their representations at this level.

We now treat D as a set of "vital" sentences and "noise" sentences. We propose *attention-pooling* to learn the sentence-level representation of D as follows: first identify vital sentences by computing attention for each of D's sentences as the cosine similarity between its representation and the query representation, then select the k highest-attention sentences to do max-pooling over them. Taking Figure 3 as an example, based on the output of the sentence-CNN layer, $k = 2$ important sentences with blue color are combined by max-pooling as the sentence-level representation $\mathbf{v}_s$ of D; the other – white-color – sentence representations are neglected as they have low attention. (If $k = all$, attention-pooling returns to the common max-pooling in (Collobert and Weston, 2008).) When the query is (Q, A), this step will be repeated, once for Q, once for A, to compute representations of D at the sentence level that are biased with respect to Q and A, respectively.

Snippet-CNN. As the example in Figure 1 shows, to answer the first question "why did Grandpa answer the door?", it does not suffice to compare this question only to the sentence "Grandpa answered the door with a smile and welcomed Jimmy inside"; instead, the snippet "Finally, Jimmy arrived at Grandpa's house and knocked. Grandpa answered the door with a smile and welcomed Jimmy inside" should be used to compare. To this end, it is necessary to stack another CNN layer, *snippet-CNN*, to learn representations of snippets, i.e., units of one or more sentences. Thus, input to snippet-CNN (resp. sentence-CNN) are sentences (resp. words) and the output is representations of snippets (resp. sentences).

Concretely, snippet-CNN puts all sentence representations in column sequence as a feature map and conducts another convolution operation over it. With filter width w, this step generates representation of snippet with w consecutive sentences. Similarly, we use the same CNN to learn higher-abstraction query representations, treating query as a document with one sentence, so that the higher-abstraction query representation is in the same space with corresponding snippet representations.

Snippet-Level Representation. For the output of snippet-CNN, each representation is more abstract and denotes bigger granularity. We apply the same attention-pooling process to snippet level representations: attention values are computed as cosine similarities between query and snippets and the snippets with the k largest attention are retained. Max-pooling over the k selected snippet representations then creates the snippet-level representation $\mathbf{v}_t$ of D. Two selected snippets are shown as red in Figure 3.

Overall Representation. Based on convolution layers at two different granularity, we have derived query-biased representations of D at sentence ($\mathbf{v}_s$) and snippet ($\mathbf{v}_t$) levels. In order to create a flexible choice for open QA, we develop a highway network (Srivastava et al., 2015) to combine the two levels of representations as an overall representation $\mathbf{v}_o$ of D:

$$\mathbf{v}_o = (1 - \mathbf{h}) \odot \mathbf{v}_s + \mathbf{h} \odot \mathbf{v}_t \tag{2}$$

where highway network weights $\mathbf{h}$ are learned by

$$\mathbf{h} = \sigma(\mathbf{W}_h \mathbf{v}_s + \mathbf{b}) \tag{3}$$

where $\mathbf{W}_h \in \mathbb{R}^{d_1 \times d_1}$. With the same highway network, we can generate the overall query representation, $\mathbf{r}_i$ in Figure 3, by combining query's representation at sentence level r_s and at snippet level r_t.

3.2 HABCNN-QP & HABCNN-QAP

HABCNN-QP/QAP computes the representation of D as a projection of D, either based on attention from Q or based on attention from A. We hope that these two projections of the document are close for a correct A and less close for an incorrect A. As we said in related work, machine comprehension can be viewed as an answer selection task *using the document D as critical background information.* Here, HABCNN-QP/QAP do not compare Q and A directly, but they use Q and A to filter the document differently, extracting what is critical for the Q/A match by attention-pooling. Then they match the two document representations in the new space.

For simplicity, we have used the symbol $\mathbf{v}_o$ so far, but in HABCNN-QP/QAP we compute two different document representations: $\mathbf{v}_{oq}$, for which attention is computed with respect to Q; and $\mathbf{v}_{oa}$ for which attention is computed with respect to A. $\mathbf{r}_i$ also has two versions, one for Q: $\mathbf{r}_{iq}$, one for A: $\mathbf{r}_{ia}$.

HABCNN-QP and HABCNN-QAP make different use of $\mathbf{v}_{oq}$. HABCNN-QAP projects D twice, once based on attention from Q, once based on attention from A and compares the two projected representations, $\mathbf{v}_{oq}$ and $\mathbf{v}_{oa}$, shown in Figure 2 (top). HABCNN-QP only utilizes the Q-based projection of D and then compares the projected document $\mathbf{v}_{oq}$ with the answer representation $\mathbf{r}_{ia}$, shown in Figure 2 (middle).

3.3 HABCNN-TE

HABCNN-TE treats machine comprehension as *textual entailment*. We use the statements that are provided in MCTest. Each statement corresponds to a question-answer pair; e.g., the Q/A pair "Why did Grandpa answer the door?" / "Because he saw the insects" (Figure 1) is reformatted into the statement "Grandpa answered the door because he saw the insects". The question answering task is then cast as: "does the document entail the statement?"

For HABCNN-TE, shown in Figure 2 (bottom), the input for Figure 3 is the pair (S, D). HABCNN-TE tries to match S's representation $\mathbf{r}_i$ with D's representation $\mathbf{v}_o$.

4 Experiments

4.1 Dataset

MCTest[1] has two subsets. MCTest-160 contains 160 items (70 train, 30 dev, 60 test), each consisting of a document, four questions followed by one correct anwer and three incorrect answers and MCTest-500 500 items (300 train, 50 dev, 150 test).

4.2 Training Setup

Our training objective is to minimize the following ranking loss function:

$$L(d, a^+, a^-) = \max(0, \alpha + S(d, a^-) - S(d, a^+)) \quad (4)$$

where $S(\cdot, \cdot)$ is a matching score between two representation vectors. Cosine similarity is used throughout. α is a constant.

Multitask learning. Based on work showing that question typing is helpful for QA (Sachan et al., 2015), we stack a logistic regression layer over question representation $\mathbf{r}_{iq}$, with the purpose that this subtask can favor the parameter tuning of the whole system, and finally the question is better recognized and answer identification is more accurate.

k	lr	d_1	bs	w	L_2	α
[1,3]	0.05	[90, 90]	1	[2,2]	0.0065	0.2

Table 1: Hyperparameters. k: top-k in attention-pooling for both CNN layers; lr: learning rate; d_1: number of kernels in CNN layers; bs: mini-batch size; w: filter width; L_2: L_2 regularization; α: constant in loss function.

To be specific, we classify questions into 12 classes: "how", "how much", "how many", "what", "who", "where", "which", "when", "whose", "why", "will" and "*other*". The question label is created by querying for the label keyword in the question. If more than one keyword appears in a question, we adopt the one appearing earlier and the more specific one (e.g., "how much", not "how"). In case there is no match, the class "*other*" is assigned.

We train with AdaGrad (Duchi et al., 2011) and use 50-dimensional GloVe embeddings (Pennington et al., 2014) to initialize word representations,[2] kept fixed during training. Table 1 gives hyperparameter values, tuned on dev.

We consider two evaluation metrics: *accuracy* (proportion of questions correctly answered) and *NDCG*$_4$ (Järvelin and Kekäläinen, 2002). Unlike accuracy which evaluates if the question is correctly answered or not, NDCG$_4$, being a measure of ranking quality, evaluates the position of the correct answer in our predicted ranking.

4.3 Baseline Systems

(i) **Addition.** Directly compare question and answers without considering the document. Sentence representations are computed by element-wise addition over word representations. (ii) **Addition-proj.** First compute sentence representations for Q, A and all D sentences as in *Addition*. Then identify two sentences from D, taking $\mathbf{x}_q$ and $\mathbf{x}_a$ as example, satisfying that they are most similar to Q and A, respectively. The match score between Q and A is then the cosine similarity of $\mathbf{x}_q$ and $\mathbf{x}_a$. (iii) **NR.** The Neural Reasoner (Peng et al., 2015) has an en-

[1] http://requery.microsoft.com/mct

[2] http://nlp.stanford.edu/projects/glove/

	method	MCTest-150						MCTest-500					
		acc			$NDCG_4$			acc			$NDCG_4$		
		one	mul	all	one	mul	all	one	mul	all	one	mul	all
Baselines	Addition	39.3	32.4	35.7	60.4	50.3	54.6	35.7	30.2	32.9	56.6	55.2	55.8
Baselines	Addition-proj	42.1	38.7	40.3	65.3	61.3	63.2	39.4	36.7	38.0	63.3	60.1	61.7
Baselines	AR	48.1	44.7	46.3	70.5	68.9	69.6	44.4	39.5	41.9	66.7	64.2	65.4
Baselines	NR	48.4	46.8	47.6	70.7	68.2	69.7	45.7	45.6	45.6	71.9	69.5	70.6
	HABCNN-QP	57.9	53.7	55.7	80.4	80.0	80.2	53.7	46.7	50.1	75.4	72.7	74.0
	HABCNN-QAP	59.0	57.9	58.4	81.5	79.9	80.6	54.0	47.2	50.6	75.7	72.6	74.1
	HABCNN-TE	**63.3**	**62.9**	**63.1**	**86.6**	**85.9**	**86.2**	**54.2**	**51.7**	**52.9**	**76.1**	**74.4**	**75.2**
	Sachan et al. (2015)	–	–	–	–	–	–	67.6	67.9	67.8	86.7	86.9	86.8
	Wang et al. (2015)	84.2	67.8	75.2	–	–	–	72.0	67.9	69.9	–	–	–

Table 2: Experimental results for one-sentence (one), multiple-sentence (mul) and all cases.

coding layer, multiple reasoning layers and a final answer layer. The input for the encoding layer is a question and the sentences of the document (called facts); each sentence is encoded by a GRU into a vector. In each reasoning layer, NR lets the question representation interact with each fact representation as reasoning process. Finally, all temporary reasoning clues are pooled as answer representation. (iv) **AR.** The Attentive Reader (Hermann et al., 2015) is implemented by modeling the whole D as a word sequence – without specific sentence / snippet representations – using an LSTM. Attention mechanism is implemented at word representation level.

Baselines Addition(-proj) do not involve complex composition and inference. NR and AR are the top-performing deep neural networks for QA.

4.4 Results

Table 2 lists the performance of baselines, HABCNN systems, and two top-performing non-DL systems (Sachan et al. (2015), Wang et al. (2015)) in the first, second, and last block, respectively. Consistently, our HABCNN systems outperform all baselines, especially surpass the two competitive DL systems AR and NR. The margin between our best-performing ABHCNN-TE and NR is 15.5/16.5 (accuracy/NDCG) on MCTest-150 and 7.3/4.6 on MCTest-500. This demonstrates the promise of our architecture in this task.

As said before, both AR and NR systems aim to *generate* answers in entity form. Their designs might not suit this machine comprehension task, in which the answers are openly-formed based on summarizing or abstracting the clues. To be more specific, AR models D always at word level, attention is also paid to corresponding word representations, which is applicable for entity-style answers, but is less suitable for comprehension at sentence level or even snippet level. NR contrarily models D in sentence level always, neglecting the discovering of key phrases which however compose most of the answers. In addition, the attention of AR system and the question-fact interaction in NR system both bring large numbers of parameters, this potentially constrains their power in a dataset of limited size.

The size of MCTest is quite small. This is the most likely reason for the inferior performance of all deep learning approaches compared to non-deep-learning approaches. If the amount of training data is limited, then it may not be possible to get top performance without a large feature engineering effort.[3]

5 Conclusion

This work takes the lead in presenting a CNN based neural network system for open-domain machine comprehension task. Our systems try to solve this task in a document projection way as well as a textual entailment way. The latter demonstrates slightly better performance. Overall, our architecture, modeling dynamic document representation by attention scheme from sentence level to snippet level, shows promising results in this task. In the future, more fine-grained representation learning approaches are expected to model complex answer types and question types.

Acknowledgments. We thank DFG for supporting this work (grant SCHU 2246/4-2).

[3]Please refer to the extended version at arxiv.org/pdf/1602.04341v1.pdf for attention visualization and error analysis.

References

Ronan Collobert and Jason Weston. 2008. A unified architecture for natural language processing: Deep neural networks with multitask learning. In *Proceedings of ICML*, pages 160–167.

John Duchi, Elad Hazan, and Yoram Singer. 2011. Adaptive subgradient methods for online learning and stochastic optimization. *The Journal of Machine Learning Research*, 12:2121–2159.

Karl Moritz Hermann, Tomas Kocisky, Edward Grefenstette, Lasse Espeholt, Will Kay, Mustafa Suleyman, and Phil Blunsom. 2015. Teaching machines to read and comprehend. In *Proceedings of NIPS*, pages 1684–1692.

Mohit Iyyer, Jordan Boyd-Graber, Leonardo Claudino, Richard Socher, and Hal Daumé III. 2014. A neural network for factoid question answering over paragraphs. In *Proceedings of EMNLP*, pages 633–644.

Kalervo Järvelin and Jaana Kekäläinen. 2002. Cumulated gain-based evaluation of ir techniques. *ACM Transactions on Information Systems (TOIS)*, 20(4):422–446.

Ankit Kumar, Ozan Irsoy, Jonathan Su, James Bradbury, Robert English, Brian Pierce, Peter Ondruska, Ishaan Gulrajani, and Richard Socher. 2016. Ask me anything: Dynamic memory networks for natural language processing. In *Proceedings of ICML*.

Karthik Narasimhan and Regina Barzilay. 2015. Machine comprehension with discourse relations. In *Proceedings ACL*, pages 1253–1262.

Baolin Peng, Zhengdong Lu, Hang Li, and Kam-Fai Wong. 2015. Towards neural network-based reasoning. *CoRR*, abs/1508.05508.

Jeffrey Pennington, Richard Socher, and Christopher D Manning. 2014. Glove: Global vectors for word representation. *Proceedings of EMNLP*, 12:1532–1543.

Matthew Richardson, Christopher JC Burges, and Erin Renshaw. 2013. Mctest: A challenge dataset for the open-domain machine comprehension of text. In *EMNLP*, volume 1, page 2.

Mrinmaya Sachan, Kumar Dubey, Eric P. Xing, and Matthew Richardson. 2015. Learning answer-entailing structures for machine comprehension. In *Proceedings of ACL*, pages 239–249.

Ellery Smith, Nicola Greco, Matko Bosnjak, and Andreas Vlachos. 2015. A strong lexical matching method for the machine comprehension test. In *Proceedings of EMNLP*, pages 1693–1698.

Rupesh K Srivastava, Klaus Greff, and Jürgen Schmidhuber. 2015. Training very deep networks. In *Proceedings of NIPS*, pages 2368–2376.

Adam Trischler, Zheng Ye, Xingdi Yuan, Jing He, Phillip Bachman, and Kaheer Suleman. 2016. A parallel-hierarchical model for machine comprehension on sparse data. *arXiv preprint arXiv:1603.08884*.

Hai Wang, Mohit Bansal, Kevin Gimpel, and David A. McAllester. 2015. Machine comprehension with syntax, frames, and semantics. In *Proceedings of ACL-IJCNLP*, pages 700–706.

Jason Weston, Antoine Bordes, Sumit Chopra, and Tomas Mikolov. 2015a. Towards ai-complete question answering: a set of prerequisite toy tasks. *arXiv preprint arXiv:1502.05698*.

Jason Weston, Sumit Chopra, and Antoine Bordes. 2015b. Memory networks. In *Proceedings of ICLR*.

Open-domain Factoid Question Answering via Knowledge Graph Search

Ahmad Aghaebrahimian, Filip Jurčíček
Charles University in Prague, Faculty of Mathematics and Physics
Institute of Formal and Applied Linguistics
Malostranské náměstí 25, 11800 Praha 1, Czech Republic
{Ebrahimian, Jurcicek}@ufal.mff.cuni.cz

Abstract

We introduce a highly scalable approach for open-domain question answering with no dependence on any data set for surface form to logical form mapping or any linguistic analytic tool such as POS tagger or named entity recognizer. We define our approach under the Constrained Conditional Models framework which lets us scale up to a full knowledge graph with no limitation on the size. On a standard benchmark, we obtained near 4 percent improvement over the state-of-the-art in open-domain question answering task.

1 Introduction

We consider the task of simple open-domain question answering. The answer to a simple question can be obtained only by knowing one entity and one property (Bordes et al., 2015).

A property is an attribute which is asked about a specific thing, place or people in a question. The thing, place or people in the question are samples of an entity. The answer to such a question is again an entity or a set of entities. For instance, in the question *"What is the time zone in Dublin?"*, Dublin is an entity and time zone is a property.

Freebase (Bollacker et al., 2008), the knowledge graph which we used in our experiments, contains about 58 million such entities and more than 14 thousands such properties. Hence, entities which we obtain from the knowledge graph are ambiguous in majority of cases. We extract metadata available in the knowledge graph and integrate them into our system using Constrained Conditional Model framework (CCM) (Roth and Yih, 2005) to disambiguate entities.

In WebQuestions (Berant et al., 2013), a data set of 5810 questions which are compiled using the Google suggest API, 86% of the questions are answerable by knowing only one entity (Bordes et al., 2015). It suggests that a large number of the questions which ordinary people ask on the Internet are simple questions and it emphasizes on the importance of simple question answering systems. Besides, the best result on this task is 63.9% (Bordes et al., 2015) which shows open-domain simple QA is still an unresolved task in NLP.

Despite the title, simple QA is not a simple task at all. Flexible and unbound number of entities and their properties in open-domain questions is an intimidating challenge for entity recognition. However, knowledge graphs by providing a structural knowledge base on entities can help a lot.

We use a knowledge graph to recognize entities at test time. Defining a model for entity disambiguation on a single question instead of a whole data set lets us to scale the system up to a large knowledge graph irrespective to its size. We elaborate on entity recognition in Sections 6.2 and 6.3.

The contributions of this paper are a highly scalable QA system and a high performance entity recognition model using knowledge graph search.

2 Related works

Domain specific QA has been studied well (Clarke et al., 2010; Kwiatkowski et al., 2010; Wong and Mooney, 2007; Zettlemoyer and Collins, 2005; Zelle and Mooney, 1996) for many domains. In majority

Proceedings of 2016 NAACL Human-Computer Question Answering Workshop, pages 22–28,
San Diego, California, June 12-17, 2016. ©2016 Association for Computational Linguistics

of these studies, a static lexicon is used for mapping surface forms of the entities to their logical forms. Scaling up such lexicons which usually contain from hundreds to several thousands entities is neither easy nor efficient. Instead, knowledge graphs contain millions of entities and are highly efficient structures which can be used for entity recognition. Knowledge graphs provide rich databases of factual information on well-known people, things and places and they proved being beneficial for different tasks in NLP including question answering.

There are many studies on using knowledge graphs for question answering either through information retrieval approach (Yao and Durme, 2014; Bordes et al., 2015) or semantic parsing (Berant et al., 2013; Berant and Liang, 2014; Cai and Yates, 2013; Kwiatkowski et al., 2013). Even in these studies, there is still a list of predefined lexicons for entity recognition (e.g., (Berant et al., 2013; Cai and Yates, 2013)). Essentially, they use knowledge graphs only for validating their generated logical forms and for entity recognition they still depend on some initial lexicons.

Dependence on predefined lexicons limits the scope of language understanding only to those predefined ones. In our approach, we don't use any data set or lexicon for entity recognition. Instead, we obtain valid entities by querying the knowledge graph at test time. Then, we apply some constraints on valid entities to get the correct entity for each question.

In part of CCM, it is first proposed by Roth and Yih in (Roth and Yih, 2005) for reasoning over classifier results. Some other people used it for different problems in NLP (Chang et al., 2012; Punyakanok et al., 2008). (Clarke et al., 2010) proposed a semantic parsing model using Question-Answering paradigm on Geoquery (Zelle, 1995) under CCM framework. Our work differs from them by the size of our data set and knowledge graph and by the open-domain nature of the questions.

The most recent work and state-of-the-art on simple QA belongs to (Bordes et al., 2015) in which they used memory networks for answering the questions in SimpleQuestions data set (Bordes et al., 2015). They proposed their system on a limited version of Freebase containing 2 and 5 million entities (FB2M, FB5M). A 0.5 % decrease in the performance of their system when scaling from FB2M to FB5M suggests that QA in a full knowledge graph is quite a difficult task. CCM lets us to scale QA from limited freebase to the full version with more than 58 million entities.

3 Knowledge graph (Freebase)

Knowledge graphs contain large amounts of factual information about entities (i.e., well-known places, people and things) and their attributes such as place of birth or profession. Large knowledge graphs generally cover numerous domains and they may be a solution for scaling up domain-dependent systems to open-domain ones by expanding their boundary of entity and property recognition. Besides, knowledge graphs are instances of the linked-data technologies. In other words, they can be connected easily to any other knowledge graph and it increases their domain of recognition.

A knowledge graph is a collection of assertions. In an assertion, a source entity is connected to a target entity through a directed and labeled edge. Large knowledge graphs such as Freebase contain billions of such assertions. The elements in an assertion (i.e., source and target entities and the connecting edge) are identified using a unique id which is called machine id or simply MID. These elements are all objects and it means they have some attributes which are called properties. The number of properties is quite huge. However, for the purpose of this paper is enough to know about *"id"*, *"mid"*, *"name"*, *"alias"*, *"type"*, and *"expected type"*.

Each entity in the graph has one unique *"id"* and one unique *"mid"*. In contrast to *"mid"* which has no meaningful association with the entity, *"id"* sometimes is meaningfully similar to its entity's surface form. *"name"* is one surface form for the respective entity and is usually a literal in form of raw text, date or a numerical value. *"alias"* contains the aliases for its entity.

Each entity has a set of *"type"*s. A *"type"* defines an *"IS A"* relation with its entity. For instance, entity *"dublin"* has types *"/topic"*, *"/book_subject"*[1], etc which says *"dublin"* not only is a general topic, but also is the name of a book.

[1] Properties are in abbreviated form to save space. For instance, the full form for this property is *"/book/book_subject"*

"expected type" is defined only for edges. It states, what you should expect to get as a target entity when traversing the graph through this edge or property. Each edge has zero or at most one expected type.

4 Constrained Conditional Model

Constrained Conditional Model (CCM) provides means of fine-tuning the results of a statistical model by enforcing declarative expressive constraints (Roth and Yih, 2005) on them. Constraints are essentially Boolean functions which can be generated using available metadata about entities and properties in Freebase. Freebase assigns a set of *"type"*s to each entity. It also assigns a unique *"expected_type"* to each property. Intuitively, the *"type"* of an answer to a question should be the same as the *"expected_type"* of the property for that question. To each test question, a set of properties each of which with different probabilities and different *"expected_type"*s is assigned. Some of the properties does not have *"expected_type"* and the types assigned to answers are not usually unique. Due to the huge number of entities and their associated types in large knowledge graphs, translating a typical constraint into a feature set for training a statistical model is practically unfeasible. However, it can be done easily using Integer Linear Programming (ILP) (Wen-tau, 2004). In this way, we simply penalize the results of a statistical model which are not in accordance with our constraints. We elaborate more on the constraints in Section 5.

5 The learning model

Let's define P and E as the space of all properties and entities respectively in a test question. For each question like *"What is the time zone in Dublin?"*, we intend to find the tuple $(p\_e) \in P \times E$ for which p's probability and e's score with respect to some features and constraints are maximal. Therefore, we would like to get *"/location/location/time_zones"*[2] as the best property and *"/en/Dublin"* as the best-matching entity in this question.

We decompose the learning model into two steps, namely; property detection and entity recognition. In property detection, we decide which property best describes the purpose of a given question. In this step, we model the assignment of properties given questions using the probability distribution in Equation 1. We use logistic regression technique to train the model and use the model for N-best property assignment to each question at test time.

$$P(p|q) = \frac{\exp(\omega_p^T \phi(q))}{\Sigma_{p_i} \exp(\omega_{p_i}^T \phi(q))} \quad (1)$$

Given a question q, the aim is to find N-best properties which best describe the content of the question and generate the correct answer when querying against the knowledge graph. ϕ in the model is a feature set representing the questions in vector space and ω are the parameters of the model.

In the second step, i.e., entity recognition, we detect and disambiguate the main entity of a question. We use an integer linear classifier for assigning the best-matching entity to each test question at test time (Equation 2). Entity recognition consists of entity detection and entity disambiguation.

$$\begin{aligned} &\text{best entity}(q) = \arg\max_e(\alpha^T s(p_q\_e_q)) \\ &(p_q\_e_p) \in P_q \times E_q \end{aligned} \quad (2)$$

A typical question usually contains tokens that all are available in the knowledge graph while only one of them is the main focus of the question. For instance, in the question *"what is the time zone in Dublin?"*, there are eleven entities which are all available in the knowledge graph (*"time, zone, time zone, ..., Dublin"*) while the focus of the question is on *"Dublin"* and we try to detect it in entity detection.

Detected entities are mostly ambiguous. Given an entity like *"Dublin"*, we need to know what Dublin (i.e., Dublin in Ireland, Dublin in Ohio, etc.) is the focus of the question. To help the system with entity disambiguation, we use heuristics as a constraint to increase the chance of correct entities. [3] Having N-best properties assigned to each question, we initial-

[2]i.e., /Type 1/Type 2/Predicate

[3]The search space in these experiments is not exponentially large hence, instead ILP, simple search methods could be used. However, this is our base line system and we are introducing more complex constraints which can not be solved by searching. To make sure our baseline system is compatible with future improvements, we used an ILP solver form the scratch.

ize $s(p_q\_e_p)$ vector. By optimizing a vector of indicator variables (α) subject to two sets of constraints, we eliminate irrelevant entities.

P_q are N-best properties for a given question q and E_q are valid entities in q. $s(p_q\_e_p)$ is a vector of p_q probabilities. α represents a vector of indicator variables which are optimized through constraint optimization. Constraints for each question are categorized into three categories:

- Constraints in the first category enforce the type of answers of $(p_q\_e_p)$ to be equal to the expected type of p_q in each question. We call the constraints in this category type constraints.
- Constraints in the second category dictate that e_p score which is lexical similarity ratio (edit distance) between the string values of *"name"* and *"id"* properties connected to an entity should be maximal. We call the constraints in this category similarity constraints.
- To make sure that the output of the entity recognition step is zero or at most one entity per question, we define the third constraint to return at most one entity.

A type constraint helps in detecting the main focus of a given question among other valid entities. Despite the assigned properties, each question has E number of valid entities. By valid we mean entities which are available in the knowledge graph.

After property detection, N-best properties are assigned to each question each of which has no or at most one *"expected_type"*. The product between the N-best properties and the E valid entities gives us $N \times E$ tuples of *(entity_ property)*. We query each tuple and obtain the respective answer from the knowledge graph. Each of the answers has a set of *"type"*s. If the *"expected_type"* of the property of each tuple was available in the set of its answer's *"type"*s, type constraint for the tuple holds true otherwise false.

A similarity constraint helps in entity disambiguation. Each entity has an *"id"* and a *"name"* properties. Ambiguous entities usually have the same *"name"* but different *"id"*s. For instance, entities *"/m/02cft"* and *"/m/013jml"* both have *"Dublin"* as their *"name"* while the *"id"* for the first one is *"/en/dublin"* and for the second one is *"/en/dublin_ohio"*(and more than 40 other different entities for the same *"name"*).

"name" assigns a surface form for entities and this is the property which we use for extracting valid entities at first place. In this case, similarity constraint for entity *"/m/02cft"* holds true because among all other entities, it has the maximal edit distance ratio between its *"name"* and *"id"* values. It is possible that the content of *"id"* property for an entity is the same as its *"mid"*. In such cases, instead *"id"*, we use *"alias"* property which contains a set of surface forms for entities.

6 Method

At training time, we have training questions accompanied with their knowledge graph assertions each of which includes an entity, a property and an answer. Entities and answers are in their MID formats. We also have access to a knowledge graph (i.e. Freebase) through an MQL query API (Google, 2013). First, all questions are fixate to 20 token. Then we chunk them into their tokens and compute $\phi(q)$ by replacing each token with its vector representation. To train our classifier, we assign a unique index to each property in the training data set and use them as label for the training questions. Given a test question at test time, we first get the N-best properties using our trained model as it is explained below.

6.1 Property detection

In property detection, we train a model which assigns N-best property to each question based on its contents. One approach for doing so is to represent the words in questions as one-hot vectors and train a classifier on them. However, representing words as discreet entities leads the classifier to disregard possible similarity between two tokens. This is known as sparsity problem and vector representation of words partially solve this problem. Word vectors or embeddings capture useful information about words and their relations to other ones. There are studies that shows there are nice directions like gender (king $\rightarrow$ queen) or even major city of countries (Germany $\rightarrow$ Berlin) in learned word vectors (Collobert et al., 2011). This attribute makes embeddings useful features for different NLP tasks specially those ones which require making decisions on the semantic contents of the texts. We use word embeddings as features in our logistics regression model instead of words themselves. It is like a one layer neural network and it is not much efficient. Still it obtained competitive results with respect to the state-of-the-art.

In another experiment, we added more layers to enhance the performance of the classifier. Finally to enhance the model even further by taking the role of neighboring words into account, we used a Convolutional Neural Network (CNN) with different filter sizes and with a max pool layer on the top. The architecture of our CNN model is similar to Yoon Kim (Kim, 2014) with some minor modifications.

The CNN model contains four consecutive layers in which the first one embeds words into low dimensional vector representation. In this step, we adopted two approaches for learning embeddings. In the first approach, we let the graph to learn word embeddings directly from data by initializing it with a random uniform distribution. In the second approach we used pre-trained Word2vec word embeddings.

The second layer in the CNN slides a convolution window with different sizes over the embeddings and the third layer max pools the result into a vector which is fed into a softmax layer for classification in the last layer. For convolution layer, we used 1,2 and 3 size windows and for the next layer we tried average and max pooling. Finally we tried 1, 2, and 3 fully connected softmax layers at the end. We trained a model in training time and then we use it to obtain N-best properties at test time. Having the properties, the next step in the model is entity recognition which includes entity detection and entity disambiguation.

6.2 Entity detection

Instead relying on external lexicons for mapping surface forms to logical forms, we match surface forms and their MIDs directly using the knowledge graph at test time. For entity detection, we extract spans in questions which are available in the knowledge graph. To do so, we slide a flexible size window over each question and extract all possible spans with all possible sizes. We query a live and full version of Freebase using Meta-Web Query Language (MQL). MQL is a template-base querying language which uses Google API service for querying Freebase on real time.

We query the entity Mid of each span against the knowledge graph. We have two alternatives to obtain initial entity Mids; greedy and full. In greedy approach, only the longest valid entities are reserved and the rest which may be still valid are disregard. In full approach, however, all the entities are reserved. For instance, in a simple span like "time zone", while greedy approach returns only *"time zone"*, full approach returns *"time"*,*"zone"* and *"time zone"*. Spans with at least one entity Mid are recognized as valid entities. Enforcing the type constraints on valid entities distinguishes relevant entities from irrelevant ones.

6.3 Entity disambiguation

Detected entities in the last step in many cases are ambiguous. Entities in large Knowledge graphs each have different meanings and interpretations. In a large knowledge graph, it is possible to find *"dublin"* as the name of a city as well as the name of a book. Moreover, when it is the name of a city, that name is not still unique as we saw in earlier section. We consider similarity constraints as true, if the lexical similarity ratio between *"id"* and *"name"* properties connected to that entity is maximal. It heuristically helps us to obtain an entity which has highest similarity with the surface form in a given question.

7 Experiment

The input for training step in our approach is training and validation sets with their knowledge graph assertions. Using Word2Vec toolkit (Mikolov et al., 2011), we replaced the tokens in the data sets with their vector representations to use them as $\phi(q)$ in our model. We pruned questions with more than 20 tokens in length and fixate shorter ones by adding extra <.> token. We already did some simple pre-processing jobs on the input data including non-alphanumeric character removal and space-separation tokens.

Using these features and the model described above, we trained a classifier using logistic regression, neural network and CNN technique. We used the trained classifier at test time for detecting 100-best properties for each test question. For multilayer

	trained on	property Acc.	over all Acc.	knowledge graph
Bordes et al.	SQ	-	61.6	FB5M
Constraint-based(LR)	SQ	69.80	61.20	Full FB
Constraint-based(NN)	SQ	74.08	63.89	Full FB
Constraint-based(CNN-1)	SQ	78.02	65.16	Full FB
Constraint-based(CNN-2)	SQ	78.82	65.19	Full FB

Table 1: Experimental results on test set of SimpleQuestions (SQ) data set. LR stands for logistic regression model, NN for neural network, CNN-1 for convolutional neural network with one channel and CNN-2 for CNN two channels model.

neural network, we used two hidden layer each with 1024 neurons and for CNN we used the same number of neurons for convolution and softmax layers. We tried to enforce regularization on weight vectors, however as already tested in (Zhang and Wallace, 2015) it had no effect on final results. We also included a new channel in our CNN using POS of tokens which improved the final model but not significantly.

The trained classifier, test questions and Freebase knowledge graph (February 2016) are inputs at test time. For testing our system, we used SimpleQuestions data set (Bordes et al., 2015) which contains 108442 factoid questions. We divided the data set into 70%, 10%, and 20% portions for train, validation and test sets respectively and we did this for three times randomly as a mean of cross validation. However, to make our result comparable to the results of SimpleQuestion authors we reported our results on the official separation test data.

For entity recognition (including detection and disambiguation), we defined two sets of constraints which are described above. Constraints in the first category (i.e., type constraints) helped with entity detection and constraints in the second category (i.e.,lexical similarity) helped with entity disambiguation. We used Gurobi solver for searching through the space of possible entities. The space of search for each question is around 100 to 500 thousands entities. With this space, Gurobi solver was able to detect entity for 20 questions per second.

We used path-level accuracy for evaluating the system. In path-level accuracy, a prediction is considered correct if the predicted entity and the property both are correct. This is the same evaluation metric which is used by the data set authors.

We obtained our best validation accuracy using greedy approach for entity recognition and 128 dimensional embeddings for property detection. Using the same configuration, we reported the accuracy of our system on test data.

8 Result

We used only SimpleQuestions to train our system and then reported the results on official test data separation (Table 1).

We reported the accuracy for property detection and overall system separately. As we mentioned earlier, in future studies we intend to work on more complex and effective constraints to improve the system performance. However, in these series of experiments, the improvement on overall system accuracy is due only to the improvement on property detection. Although our system makes query on the whole knowledge graph, to make sure our results are comparable, we eliminate entities which are not available in FB5M. In this settings, with 99% coverage, we obtained 61.2% accuracy in our logistics regression model which is competitive to the results in (Bordes et al., 2015) when training on the same data set (61.6%). Our neural network system obtained 63.89 which is the same with (Bordes et al., 2015) best results when they trained on three training data sets (WebQuestions and paraphrase data sets in addition to Simple Question). Finally our CNN model obtained 65.19% accuracy only trained on SimpleQuestions. Since we work on full knowledge graph, we hope that our system can answer every possible simple question which its answer is available in the full knowledge graph but not in the FB2M.

9 Conclusion

We introduced a question answering system with no dependence on external lexicons or any other tool. Using our system and on a full knowledge graph, we obtained state-of-the-art results on simple question answering task without any linguistic analytic tool or lexicon. By means of enforcing expressive constraint on statistical models, our approach is able to easily scale up QA systems to a large knowledge graph irrespective to its size.

Acknowledgments

This research was partially funded by the Ministry of Education, Youth and Sports of the Czech Republic under the grant agreement LK11221, core research funding, SVV project number 260 333 and GAUK 207-10/250098 of Charles University in Prague. This work has been using language resources distributed by the LINDAT/CLARIN project of the Ministry of Education, and Sports of the Czech Republic (project LM2010013).

References

J. Berant and P. Liang. 2014. Semantic parsing via paraphrasing. *In Proceedings of Association for Computational Linguistics.*

J. Berant, A. Chou, R. Frostig, and P. Liang. 2013. Semantic parsing on freebase from question-answer pairs. *In Proceedings of Empirical Methods in Natural Language Processing.*

K. Bollacker, C. Evans, P. Paritosh, T. Sturge, and J. Taylor. 2008. a collaboratively created graph database for structuring human knowledge. *In Proceedings of the 2008 ACM SIGMOD international conference on Management of data.*

A. Bordes, N. Usunier, S. Chopra, and J. Weston. 2015. Large-scale simple question answering with memory networks. *In arXiv preprint arXiv:1506.02075.*

Q. Cai and A. Yates. 2013. Large-scale semantic parsing via schema matching and lexicon extension. *In Proceedings of of Association for Computational Linguistics.*

M. Chang, L. Ratinov, and D. Roth. 2012. Structured learning with constrained conditional models. *Machine Learning.*

J. Clarke, D. Goldwasser, M. Chang, and D. Roth. 2010. Driving semantic parsing from the world's response. *In Proceedings of the Conference on Computational Natural Language Learning.*

R. Collobert, J. Weston, L. Bottou, M. Karlen, K. Kavukcuoglu, and P. kuksa. 2011. Natural language processing (almost) from scratch. *Machine Learning Research.*

Google. 2013. Freebase data dumps.

Y. Kim. 2014. Convolutional neural networks for sentence classification. *In Proceedings of EMNLP.*

T. Kwiatkowski, L. Zettlemoyer, S. Goldwater, and M. Steedman. 2010. Inducing probabilistic ccg grammars from logical form with higher-order unification. *In Proceedings of the Conference on Empirical Methods in Natural Language Processing.*

T. Kwiatkowski, C. Eunsol, Y. Artzi, and L. Zettlemoyer. 2013. Scaling semantic parsers with on-the-fly ontology matching. *In Proceedings of the Conference on Empirical Methods in Natural Language Processing.*

T. Mikolov, S. Kombrink, A. Deoras, L. Burget, and J. Černocký. 2011. Rnnlm - recurrent neural network language modeling toolkit.

V. Punyakanok, D. Roth, and W. Yih. 2008. The importance of syntactic parsing and inference in semantic role labeling. *Computational Linguistics.*

D. Roth and W. Yih. 2005. Integer linear programing inference for conditional random fields. *International Conference on Machine Learning.*

Y. Wen-tau. 2004. Global inference using integer linear programming.

Y-W. Wong and R. Mooney. 2007. Learning synchronous grammars for semantic parsing with lambda calculus. *In Proceedings of Association for Computational Linguistics.*

X. Yao and B. Van Durme. 2014. Information extraction over structured data: Question answering with freebase. *In Proceedings of Association for Computational Linguistics.*

J. M. Zelle and R. J. Mooney. 1996. Learning to parse database queries using inductive logic proramming. *In Proceedings of the National Conference on Artificial Intelligence.*

J. M. Zelle. 1995. Using inductive logic programming to automate the construction of natural language parsers. *Ph.D. thesis, Department of Computer Sciences, The University of Texas at Austin.*

L. Zettlemoyer and M. Collins. 2005. Learning to map sentences to logical form: Structured classification with probabilistic categorial grammars. *In Proceedings of the Annual Conference in Uncertainty in Artificial Intelligence (UAI).*

Y. Zhang and B. C. Wallace. 2015. A sensitivity analysis of (and practitioners' guide to) convolutional neural networks for sentence classification. *arXiv preprint arXiv:1510.03820.*

Neural Enquirer: Learning to Query Tables in Natural Language

Pengcheng Yin
The University of Hong Kong
pcyin@cs.hku.hk

Zhengdong Lu
Huawei Noah's Ark Lab
Lu.Zhengdong@huawei.com

Hang Li
Huawei Noah's Ark Lab
HangLi.HL@huawei.com

Ben Kao
The University of Hong Kong
kao@cs.hku.hk

Abstract

We propose NEURAL ENQUIRER — a neural network architecture for answering natural language (NL) questions given a knowledge base (KB) table. Unlike previous work on end-to-end training of semantic parsers, NEURAL ENQUIRER is fully "neuralized": it gives distributed representations of queries and KB tables, and executes queries through a series of differentiable operations. The model can be trained with gradient descent using both end-to-end and step-by-step supervision. During training the representations of queries and the KB table are jointly optimized with the query execution logic. Our experiments show that the model can learn to execute complex NL queries on KB tables with rich structures.

1 Introduction

Natural language dialogue and question answering often involve querying a knowledge base (Wen et al., 2015; Berant et al., 2013). The traditional approach involves two steps: First, a given query $\tilde{Q}$ is semantically parsed into an "executable" representation, which is often expressed in certain logical form $\tilde{Z}$ (e.g., SQL-like queries). Second, the representation is executed against a KB from which an answer is obtained. For queries that involve complex semantics and logic (e.g., "*Which city hosted the longest Olympic Games before the Games in Beijing?*"), semantic parsing and query execution become extremely complex. For example, carefully hand-crafted features and rules are needed to correctly parse a complex query into its logical form (see example in the lower-left corner of Figure 1). To partially overcome this complexity, recent works (Clarke et al., 2010; Liang et al., 2011; Pasupat and Liang, 2015) attempt to "backpropagate" query execution results to revise the semantic representation of a query. This approach, however, is greatly hindered by the fact that traditional semantic parsing mostly involves rule-based features and symbolic manipulation, and is subject to intractable search space incurred by the great flexibility of natural language.

In this paper we propose NEURAL ENQUIRER — a neural network system that learns to understand NL queries and execute them on a KB table from examples of queries and answers. Unlike similar efforts along this line of research (Neelakantan et al., 2015), NEURAL ENQUIRER is a fully neuralized, end-to-end differentiable network that jointly models semantic parsing and query execution. It encodes queries and KB tables into distributed representations, and executes compositional queries against the KB through a series of differentiable operations. The model is trained using query-answer pairs, where the distributed representations of queries and the KB are optimized together with the query execution logic in an end-to-end fashion. We demonstrate using a synthetic QA task that NEURAL ENQUIRER is capable of learning to execute complex compositional NL questions.

2 Model

Given an NL query Q and a KB table $\mathcal{T}$, NEURAL ENQUIRER executes Q against $\mathcal{T}$ and outputs a ranked list of answers. The execution is done by first

Proceedings of 2016 NAACL Human-Computer Question Answering Workshop, pages 29–35,
San Diego, California, June 12-17, 2016. ©2016 Association for Computational Linguistics

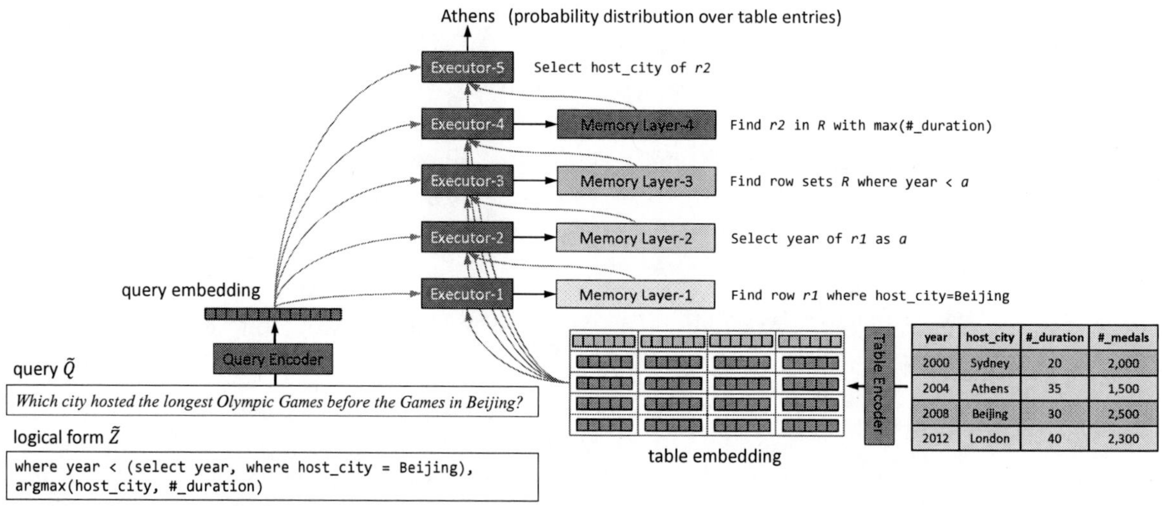

Figure 1: An overview of NEURAL ENQUIRER with five executors

using *Encoders* to encode the query and table into distributed representations, which are then sent to a cascaded pipeline of *Executors* to derive the answer. Figure 1 gives an illustrative example. It consists of the following components:

2.1 Query Encoder

Query Encoder abstracts the semantics of an NL query Q and encodes it into a query embedding $\mathbf{q} \in \mathbb{R}^{d_Q}$. Let $\{\mathbf{x}_1, \mathbf{x}_2, \ldots, \mathbf{x}_T\}$ be the embeddings of the words in Q, where $\mathbf{x}_t \in \mathbb{R}^{d_W}$ is from an embedding matrix $\mathbf{L}$. We employ a bidirectional Gated Recurrent Unit (GRU) (Bahdanau et al., 2015) to summarize the sequence of word embeddings in forward and reverse orders. $\mathbf{q}$ is formed by concatenating the last hidden states in the two directions.

We remark that Query Encoder can find the representation of a rather general class of symbol sequences, agnostic to the actual representation of the query (e.g., natural language, SQL, etc). The model is able to learn the semantics of input queries through end-to-end training, making it a generic model for query understanding and query execution.

2.2 Table Encoder

Table Encoder converts a KB table $\mathcal{T}$ into a distributed representation, which is used as an input to executors. Suppose $\mathcal{T}$ has M rows and N columns. In our model, the n-th column is associated with a *field name* (e.g., `host_city`). Each cell value is a word (e.g., *Beijing*) in the vocabulary. We use w_{mn} to denote the cell value in row m column n, and $\mathbf{w}_{mn}$ to denote its embedding. Let $\mathbf{f}_n$ be the embedding of the field name for column n. For each entry (cell) w_{mn}, Table Encoder computes a ⟨field, value⟩ composite embedding $\mathbf{e}_{mn} \in \mathbb{R}^{d_\mathcal{E}}$ by fusing $\mathbf{f}_n$ and $\mathbf{w}_{mn}$ through a non-linear transformation:

$$\mathbf{e}_{mn} = \tanh(\mathbf{W} \cdot [\mathbf{f}_n; \mathbf{w}_{mn}] + \mathbf{b}),$$

where $[\cdot;\cdot]$ denotes vector concatenation. The output of Table Encoder is an $M \times N \times d_\mathcal{E}$ tensor that consists of $M \times N$ embeddings, each of length $d_\mathcal{E}$.

2.3 Executor

NEURAL ENQUIRER executes an input query on a KB table through layers of execution. Each layer consists of an executor that, after learning, performs certain operation (e.g., `select`, `max`) relevant to the input query. An executor outputs intermediate execution results, referred to as *annotations*, which are saved in the external memory of the executor. A query is executed sequentially through a stack of executors. Such a cascaded architecture enables the model to answer complex, compositional queries. An example is given in Figure 1 in which descriptions of the operation each executor is assumed to perform for the query $\tilde{Q}$ are shown. We will demonstrate in Section 4 that the model is capable of learning the operation logic of each executor via end-to-end training.

As illustrated in Figure 2, an executor at Layer-ℓ (denoted as Executor-ℓ) consists of two major neural network components: a *Reader* and an *Annotator*. The executor processes a table row-by-row. The

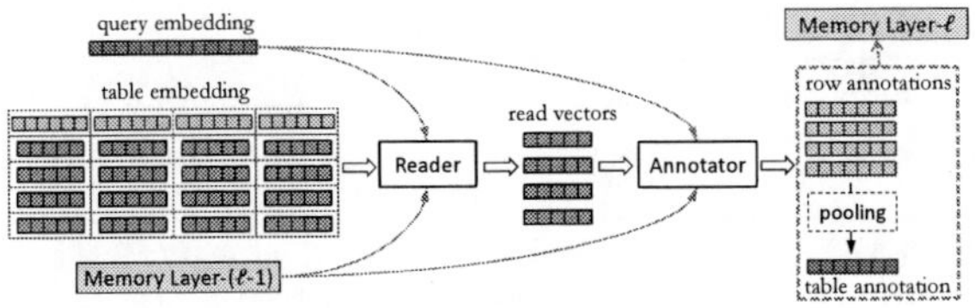

Figure 2: Overview of an Executor-ℓ

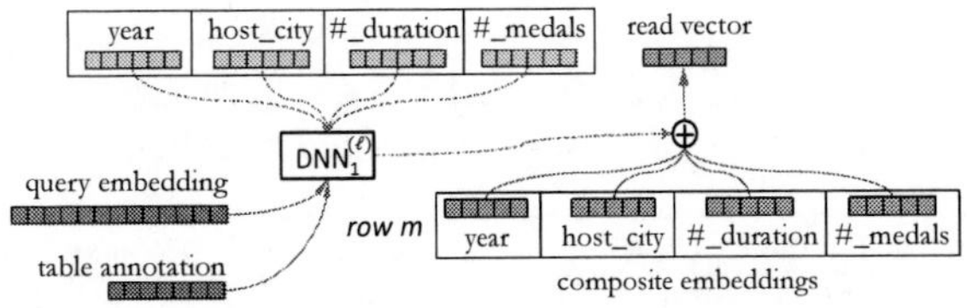

Figure 3: Illustration of the Reader in Executor-ℓ.

Reader reads in data from each row m in the form of a *read vector* $\mathbf{r}_m^\ell$, which is then sent to the Annotator to perform the actual execution. The output of the Annotator is a *row annotation* $\mathbf{a}_m^\ell$, which captures the row-wise local computation result. Once all row annotations are obtained, Executor-ℓ generates a *table annotation* $\mathbf{g}^\ell$ to summarize the global computation result on the whole table by pooling all row annotations. All the row and table annotations are saved in the memory of Layer-ℓ: $\mathcal{M}^\ell = \{\mathbf{a}_1^\ell, \mathbf{a}_2^\ell, \ldots, \mathbf{a}_M^\ell, \mathbf{g}^\ell\}$. Intuitively, row annotations handle operations that require only row-wise, local information (e.g., `select`, `where`), while table annotations model superlative operations (e.g., `max`, `min`) by aggregating table-wise, global execution results. A combination of row and table annotations enables the model to perform a wide variety of query operations in real world scenarios.

2.3.1 Reader

As illustrated in Figure 3, for the m-th row with N $\langle$field, value$\rangle$ composite embeddings $\mathcal{R}_m = \{\mathbf{e}_{m1}, \mathbf{e}_{m2}, \ldots, \mathbf{e}_{mN}\}$, the Reader fetches a read vector $\mathbf{r}_m^\ell$ from $\mathcal{R}_m$ via an attentive reading operation:

$$\mathbf{r}_m^\ell = f_{\mathrm{R}}^\ell(\mathcal{R}_m, \mathcal{F}_\mathcal{T}, \mathbf{q}, \mathcal{M}^{\ell-1}) = \sum_{n=1}^{N} \tilde{\omega}(\mathbf{f}_n, \mathbf{q}, \mathbf{g}^{\ell-1})\mathbf{e}_{mn}$$

where $\mathcal{M}^{\ell-1}$ denotes the content of memory Layer-$(\ell-1)$, and $\mathcal{F}_\mathcal{T} = \{\mathbf{f}_1, \mathbf{f}_2, \ldots, \mathbf{f}_N\}$ is the set of field name embeddings. $\tilde{\omega}(\cdot)$ is the normalized attention weights given by:

$$\tilde{\omega}(\mathbf{f}_n, \mathbf{q}, \mathbf{g}^{\ell-1}) = \frac{\exp(\omega(\mathbf{f}_n, \mathbf{q}, \mathbf{g}^{\ell-1}))}{\sum_{n'=1}^{N} \exp(\omega(\mathbf{f}_{n'}, \mathbf{q}, \mathbf{g}^{\ell-1}))} \quad (1)$$

where $\omega(\cdot)$ is modeled as a Deep Neural Network (denoted as $\mathsf{DNN}_1^{(\ell)}$). Since each executor models a specific type of computation, it should only attend to a subset of entries that are pertinent to its execution. This is modeled by the Reader. Our approach is related to the content-based addressing of Neural Turing Machines (Graves et al., 2014) and the attention mechanism in neural machine translation models (Bahdanau et al., 2015).

2.3.2 Annotator

The Annotator of Executor-ℓ computes row and table annotations based on read vectors fetched by the Reader. The results are stored in the ℓ-th memory layer $\mathcal{M}^\ell$ accessible to Executor-$(\ell{+}1)$. The last executor is the only exception, which outputs the final answer.

[Row annotations] Capturing row-wise execution result, the annotation $\mathbf{a}_m^\ell$ for row m in Executor-ℓ is given by

$$\mathbf{a}_m^\ell = f_{\mathrm{A}}^\ell(\mathbf{r}_m^\ell, \mathbf{q}, \mathcal{M}^{\ell-1}) = \mathsf{DNN}_2^{(\ell)}([\mathbf{r}_m^\ell; \mathbf{q}; \mathbf{a}_m^{\ell-1}; \mathbf{g}^{\ell-1}]).$$

$\mathsf{DNN}_2^{(\ell)}$ fuses the corresponding read vector $\mathbf{r}_m^\ell$, the results saved in the previous memory layer (row and table annotations $\mathbf{a}_m^{\ell-1}$, $\mathbf{g}^{\ell-1}$), and the query embedding $\mathbf{q}$. Specifically,

- row annotation $\mathbf{a}_m^{\ell-1}$ represents the local status of execution before Layer-ℓ;
- table annotation $\mathbf{g}^{\ell-1}$ summarizes the global status of execution before Layer-ℓ;
- read vector $\mathbf{r}_m^\ell$ stores the value of attentive reading;
- query embedding $\mathbf{q}$ encodes the overall execution agenda.

All the above values are combined through $\mathsf{DNN}_2^{(\ell)}$ to form the annotation of row m in the current layer.

[Table annotations] Capturing global execution state, a table annotation summarizes all row annotations via a global max pooling operation:

$$\mathbf{g}^\ell = f_{\mathrm{MaxPool}}(\mathbf{a}_1^\ell, \mathbf{a}_2^\ell, \ldots, \mathbf{a}_M^\ell) = [g_1, g_2, \ldots, g_{d_G}]^\top$$

year	host_city	#_participants	#_medals	#_duration	#_audience	host_country	GDP	country_size	population
2008	Beijing	4,200	2,500	30	67,000	China	2,300	960	130

Figure 4: An example table in the synthetic QA task (only one row shown)

① SELECT_WHERE `[select Fa, where Fb = wb]`	③ WHERE_SUPERLATIVE `[where Fa >|< wa, argmax/min(Fb, Fc)]`
▷ *How many people participated in the game in Beijing?* ▷ *In which city was the game hosted in 2012?*	▷ *How long was the game with the most medals that had fewer than 3,000 participants?* ▷ *How many medals were in the first game after 2008?*
② SUPERLATIVE `[argmax/min(Fa, Fb)]`	④ NEST `[where Fa >|< (select Fa,where Fb=wb), argmax/min(Fc, Fd)]`
▷ *When was the latest game hosted?* ▷ *How big is the country which hosted the shortest game?*	▷ *Which country hosted the longest game before the game in Athens?* ▷ *How many people watched the earliest game that lasts for more days than the game in 1956?*

Table 1: Example queries for each query type, with annotated SQL-like logical form templates

where $g_k = \max(\{\mathbf{a}_1^\ell(k), \mathbf{a}_2^\ell(k), \ldots, \mathbf{a}_M^\ell(k)\})$ is the maximum value among the k-th elements of all row annotations.

2.3.3 Last Layer Executor

Instead of computing annotations based on read vectors, the last executor in NEURAL ENQUIRER directly outputs the probability of an entry w_{mn} in table $\mathcal{T}$ being the answer a:

$$p(a = w_{mn}|Q, \mathcal{T}) = \frac{\exp(f_{\text{ANS}}^\ell(\mathbf{e}_{mn}, \mathbf{q}, \mathbf{a}_m^{\ell-1}, \mathbf{g}^{\ell-1}))}{\sum_{m'=1,n'=1}^{M,N} \exp(f_{\text{ANS}}^\ell(\mathbf{e}_{m'n'}, \mathbf{q}, \mathbf{a}_{m'}^{\ell-1}, \mathbf{g}^{\ell-1}))} \quad (2)$$

where $f_{\text{ANS}}^\ell(\cdot)$ is modeled as a DNN ($\text{DNN}_3^{(\ell)}$). Note that the last executor, which is devoted to returning answers, could still carry out execution in $\text{DNN}_3^{(\ell)}$.

3 Learning

NEURAL ENQUIRER can be trained in an *end-to-end* (N2N) fashion. Given a set of $N_\mathcal{D}$ query-table-answer triples $\mathcal{D} = \{(Q^{(i)}, \mathcal{T}^{(i)}, y^{(i)})\}$, the model is optimized by maximizing the log-likelihood of gold-standard answers:

$$\mathcal{L}_{\text{N2N}}(\mathcal{D}) = \sum_{i=1}^{N_\mathcal{D}} \log p(a = y^{(i)}|Q^{(i)}, \mathcal{T}^{(i)}) \quad (3)$$

The training can also be carried out with stronger guidance, i.e., *step-by-step* (SbS) supervision, by softly guiding the learning process via controlling the attention weights $\tilde{w}(\cdot)$ in Eq. (1). As an example, for Executor-1 in Figure 1, by biasing the attention weight of the `host_city` field towards 1.0, only the value of `host_city` will be fetched and sent to the Annotator. In this way we can "force" the executor to learn the `where` operation to find the row whose `host_city` is *Beijing*. Formally, this is done by introducing additional supervision signal to Eq. (3):

$$\mathcal{L}_{\text{SbS}}(\mathcal{D}) = \sum_{i=1}^{N_\mathcal{D}} [\log p(a = y^{(i)}|Q^{(i)}, \mathcal{T}^{(i)}) + \alpha \sum_{\ell=1}^{L-1} \log \tilde{w}(\mathbf{f}_{i,\ell}^\star, \cdot, \cdot)] \quad (4)$$

where α is a tuning weight, and L is the number of executors. $\mathbf{f}_{i,\ell}^\star$ is the embedding of the field known *a priori* to be used by Executor-ℓ in answering the i-th example.

4 Experiments

In this section we evaluate NEURAL ENQUIRER on synthetic QA tasks with NL queries of varying compositional depths.

4.1 Synthetic QA Task

We present a synthetic QA task with a large number of QA examples at various levels of complexity to evaluate the performance of NEURAL ENQUIRER. Starting with "artificial" tasks accelerates the development of novel deep models (Weston et al., 2015), and has gained increasing popularity in recent research on modeling symbolic computation using DNNs (Graves et al., 2014; Zaremba and Sutskever, 2014).

Our synthetic dataset consists of query-table-answer triples $\{(Q^{(i)}, \mathcal{T}^{(i)}, y^{(i)})\}$. To generate a triple, we first randomly sample a table $\mathcal{T}^{(i)}$ of size 10×10 from a synthetic schema of Olympic Games. The cell values of $\mathcal{T}^{(i)}$ are drawn from a vocabulary of 120 location names and 120 numbers. Figure 4 gives an example table. Next, we sample a query $Q^{(i)}$ generated using NL templates, and obtain its gold-standard answer $y^{(i)}$ on $\mathcal{T}^{(i)}$. Our task consists of four types of NL queries, with examples given in Table 1. We also give the logical form template

	MIXED-25K			MIXED-100K	
	SEMPRE	N2N	SbS	N2N	SbS
SELECT_WHERE	93.8%	96.2%	99.7%	99.3%	100.0%
SUPERLATIVE	97.8%	98.9%	99.5%	99.9%	100.0%
WHERE_SUPERLATIVE	34.8%	80.4%	94.3%	98.5%	99.8%
NEST	34.4%	60.5%	92.1%	64.7%	99.7%
Overall Accuracy	65.2%	84.0%	96.4%	90.6%	99.9%

Table 2: Accuracies on MIXED datasets

for each type of query. The templates define the semantics and compositionality of queries. We generate queries at various compositional depths, ranging from simple SELECT_WHERE queries to more complex NEST ones. This makes the dataset have similar complexity as a real-world one, except for the relatively small vocabulary. The queries are flexible enough to involve complex matching between NL phrases and logical constituents, which makes query understanding nontrivial: (1) the same field is described by different NL phrases (e.g., *"How big is the country ..."* and *"What is the size of the country ..."* for the `country_size` field); (2) different fields may be referred to by the same NL pattern (e.g, *"in China"* for `host_country` and *"in Beijing"* for `host_city`); (3) simple NL constituents may be grounded to complex logical operations (e.g., *"after the game in Beijing"* implies comparing between the values of `year` fields).

To simulate the read-world scenario where queries of various types are issued to the model, we construct two MIXED datasets, with $25K$ and $100K$ training examples respectively, where four types of queries are sampled with the ratio $1:1:1:2$. Both datasets share the same testing set of $20K$ examples, $5K$ for each type of query. We enforce that no tables and queries are shared between training/testing sets.

4.2 Setup

[Tuning] We adopt a model with five executors. The lengths of hidden states for GRU and DNNs are 150, 50. The numbers of layers for $\mathsf{DNN}_1^{(\ell)}$, $\mathsf{DNN}_2^{(\ell)}$ and $\mathsf{DNN}_3^{(\ell)}$ are 2, 3, 3. The length of word embeddings and annotations is 20. α is 0.2. We train the model using ADADELTA (Zeiler, 2012) on a Tesla K40 GPU. The training converges fast within 2 hours.

[Metric] We evaluate in terms of accuracy, defined as the fraction of correctly answered queries.

[Models] We compare the results of the following settings:

- **Sempre** (Pasupat and Liang, 2015) is a state-of-the-art semantic parser and serves as the baseline;
- **N2N**, NEURAL ENQUIRER model trained using *end-to-end* setting (Sec 4.3);
- **SbS**, NEURAL ENQUIRER model trained using *step-by-step* setting (Sec 4.4).

4.3 End-to-End Evaluation

Table 2 summarizes the results of SEMPRE and NEURAL ENQUIRER under different settings. We show both the individual performance for each query type and the overall accuracy. We evaluate SEMPRE only on MIXED-25K because of its long training time even on this small dataset (about 3 days).

In this section we discuss the results under end-to-end (N2N) training setting. On MIXED-25K, the relatively low performance of SEMPRE indicates that our QA task, although synthetic, is highly nontrivial. Surprisingly, our model outperforms SEMPRE on all types of queries, with a marginal gain on *simple* queries (SELECT_WHERE, SUPERLATIVE), and significant improvement on *complex* queries (WHERE_SUPERLATIVE, NEST). On MIXED-100K, our model achieves a decent overall accuracy of 90.6%. These results show that in our QA task, NEURAL ENQUIRER is very effective in answering compositional NL queries, especially those with complex semantic structures compared with the state-of-the-art system.

To further understand why our model is capable of answering compositional queries, we study the attention weights $\tilde{w}(\cdot)$ of Readers (Eq. 1) for executors in intermediate layers, and the answer probability (Eq. 2) the last executor outputs for each entry in the table. Those statistics are obtained on MIXED-100K. We sample two queries (Q_1 and Q_2) in the testing set that our model answers correctly and visualize their corresponding values in Figure 5. To

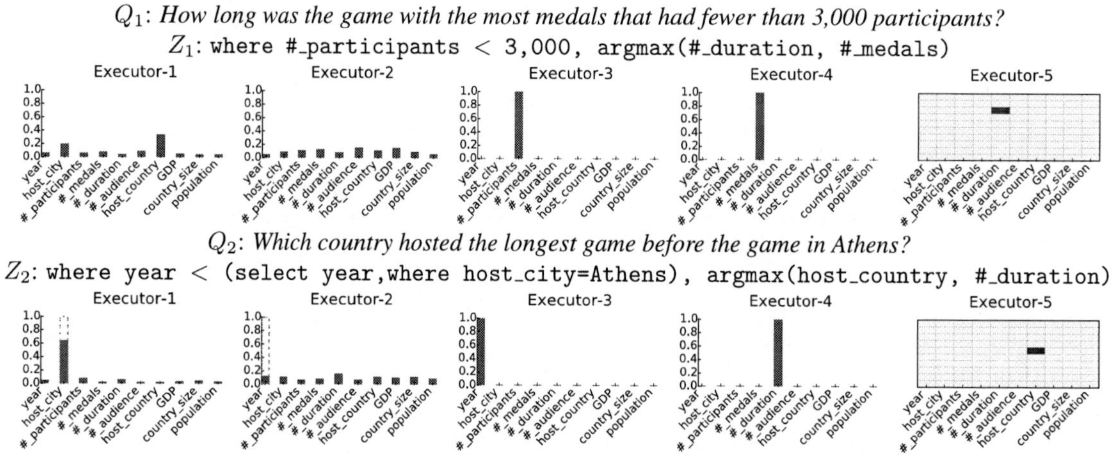

Figure 5: Weights visualization of queries Q_1 and Q_2

better understand the query execution process, we also give the logical forms (Z_1 and Z_2) of the two queries. Note that the logical forms are just for reference purpose and unknown by the model. We find that each executor actually *learns* its execution logic from just the correct answers in N2N training, which is in accordance with our assumption. The model executes Q_1 in three steps, with each of the last three executors performs a specific type of operation. For each row, Executor-3 takes the value of the `#_participants` field as input, while Executor-4 attends to the `#_medals` field. Finally, Executor-5 outputs a high probability for the `#_duration` field in the 3-rd row. The attention weights for Executor-1 and Executor-2 appear to be meaningless because Q_1 requires only three steps of execution, and the model learns to defer the meaningful execution to the last three executors. Compared with the logical form Z_1 of Q_1, we can deduce that Executor-3 "executes" the `where` clause in Z_1 to find row sets R satisfying the condition, and Executor-4 performs the first part of `argmax` to find the row $r \in R$ with the maximum value of `#_medals`, while Executor-5 outputs the value of `#_duration` in row r.

Compared with Q_1, Q_2 is more complicated. According to Z_2, Q_2 involves an additional nest sub-query to be solved by two extra executors, and requires a total of five steps of execution. The last three executors function similarly as in answering Q_1, yet the execution logic for the first two executors (devoted to solving the sub-query) is a bit obscure, since their attention weights are scattered instead of being perfectly centered on the ideal fields as highlighted in red dashed rectangles. We posit that this is because during the end-to-end training, the supervision signal propagated from the top layer has decayed along the long path down to the first two executors, which causes vanishing gradients.

4.4 With Additional Step-by-Step Supervision

To alleviate the vanishing gradient problem when training on complex queries like Q_2, we train the model using step-by-step (SbS) setting (Eq. 4), where we encourage each intermediate executor to attend to the field that is known *a priori* to be relevant to its execution logic. Results are shown in Table 2 (column SbS). With stronger supervision signal, the model significantly outperforms the N2N setting, and achieves perfect accuracy on MIXED-100K. This shows that NEURAL ENQUIRER is capable of leveraging the additional supervision signal given to intermediate layers in SbS training. Let us revisit the query Q_2 in SbS setting. In contrast to the result in N2N setting (Figure 5) where the attention weights for the first two executors are obscure, now the weights are perfectly skewed towards each relevant field with a value of 1.0, which corresponds with the highlighted ideal weights.

5 Conclusion

We propose NEURAL ENQUIRER, a fully neural, end-to-end differentiable network that learns to execute compositional natural language queries on knowledge-base tables.

References

[Bahdanau et al.2015] Dzmitry Bahdanau, Kyunghyun Cho, and Yoshua Bengio. 2015. Neural machine translation by jointly learning to align and translate. In *ICLR*.

[Berant et al.2013] Jonathan Berant, Andrew Chou, Roy Frostig, and Percy Liang. 2013. Semantic parsing on freebase from question-answer pairs. In *EMNLP*, pages 1533–1544.

[Clarke et al.2010] James Clarke, Dan Goldwasser, Ming-Wei Chang, and Dan Roth. 2010. Driving semantic parsing from the world's response. In *CoNLL*, pages 18–27.

[Graves et al.2014] Alex Graves, Greg Wayne, and Ivo Danihelka. 2014. Neural turing machines. *CoRR*, abs/1410.5401.

[Liang et al.2011] Percy Liang, Michael I. Jordan, and Dan Klein. 2011. Learning dependency-based compositional semantics. In *ACL (1)*, pages 590–599.

[Neelakantan et al.2015] Arvind Neelakantan, Quoc V. Le, and Ilya Sutskever. 2015. Neural programmer: Inducing latent programs with gradient descent. *CoRR*, abs/1511.04834.

[Pasupat and Liang2015] Panupong Pasupat and Percy Liang. 2015. Compositional semantic parsing on semi-structured tables. In *ACL (1)*, pages 1470–1480.

[Wen et al.2015] Tsung-Hsien Wen, Milica Gasic, Nikola Mrksic, Pei hao Su, David Vandyke, and Steve J. Young. 2015. Semantically conditioned lstm-based natural language generation for spoken dialogue systems. In *EMNLP*, pages 1711–1721.

[Weston et al.2015] Jason Weston, Antoine Bordes, Sumit Chopra, and Tomas Mikolov. 2015. Towards ai-complete question answering: A set of prerequisite toy tasks. *CoRR*, abs/1502.05698.

[Zaremba and Sutskever2014] Wojciech Zaremba and Ilya Sutskever. 2014. Learning to execute. *CoRR*, abs/1410.4615.

[Zeiler2012] Matthew D. Zeiler. 2012. ADADELTA: an adaptive learning rate method. *CoRR*, abs/1212.5701.

Neural Generative Question Answering

Jun Yin[1]* **Xin Jiang**[2] **Zhengdong Lu**[2], **Lifeng Shang**[2], **Hang Li**[2], **Xiaoming Li**[1]
[1]School of Electronic Engineering and Computer Science, Peking University
[2]Noah's Ark Lab, Huawei Technologies
{jun.yin,lxm}@pku.edu.cn, {jiang.xin, lu.zhengdong, shang.lifeng, hangli.hl}@huawei.com

Abstract

This paper presents an end-to-end neural network model, named Neural Generative Question Answering (GENQA), that can generate answers to *simple factoid questions*, based on the facts in a knowledge-base. More specifically, the model is built on the encoder-decoder framework for sequence-to-sequence learning, while equipped with the ability to enquire the knowledge-base, and is trained on a corpus of question-answer pairs, with their associated triples in the knowledge-base. Empirical study shows the proposed model can effectively deal with the variations of questions and answers, and generate right and natural answers by referring to the facts in the knowledge-base. The experiment on question answering demonstrates that the proposed model can outperform an embedding-based QA model as well as a neural dialogue model trained on the same data.

1 Introduction

Question answering (QA) can be viewed as a special case of single-turn dialogue: QA aims at providing correct answers to the questions in natural language, while dialogue emphasizes on generating relevant and fluent responses to the messages also in natural language (Shang et al., 2015; Vinyals and Le, 2015). Recent progress in deep learning has raised the possibility of realizing generation-based QA in a purely neutralized way. That is, the answer is generated by a neural network (e.g., recurrent neural network, or RNN) based on the question, which is able to handle the flexibility and diversity of language. More importantly, the model is trained in an end-to-end fashion, and thus there is no need in building the system using linguistic knowledge, e.g., creating a semantic parser.

There is however one serious limitation of this generation-based approach to QA. It is practically impossible to store all the knowledge in a neural network to achieve a desired precision and coverage in real world QA. This is a fundamental difficulty, rooting deeply in the way in which knowledge is acquired, represented and stored. The neural network, and more generally the fully distributed way of representation, is good at representing smooth and shared patterns, i.e., modeling the flexibility and diversity of language, but improper for representing discrete and isolated concepts, i.e., depicting the lexicon of language.

On the other hand, the recent success of memory-based neural network models has greatly extended the ways of storing and accessing text information, in both short-term memory (e.g., in (Bahdanau et al., 2015)) and long-term memory (e.g., in (Weston et al., 2015)). It is hence a natural choice to connect a neural model for QA with a neural model of knowledge-base on an external memory, which is also related to the traditional approach of template-based QA from knowledge-base.

In this paper, we report our exploration in this direction, with a proposed model called *Neural Generative Question Answering* (GENQA).

Learning Task: We formalize generative question answering (GENQA) as a supervised learning task or

* The work is done when the first author worked as intern at Noah's Ark Lab, Huawei Technologies.

Proceedings of 2016 NAACL Human-Computer Question Answering Workshop, pages 36–42,
San Diego, California, June 12-17, 2016.

Table 1: Examples of training instances for GENQA. The KB-words in the training instances are underlined in the examples.

Question & Answer	Triple (*subject, predicate, object*)
Q: *How tall is Yao Ming?* A: *He is <u>2.29m</u> and is visible from space.*	`(Yao Ming, height, 2.29m)`
Q: *Which country was Beethoven from?* A: *He was born in what is now <u>Germany</u>.*	`(Ludwig van Beethoven, place of birth, Germany)`
Q: *Which club does Messi play for?* A: *Lionel Messi currently plays for <u>FC Barcelona</u> in the Spanish Primera Liga.*	`(Lionel Messi, team, FC Barcelon)`

more specifically a sequence-to-sequence learning task. A GENQA system takes a sequence of words as input question and generates another sequence of words as answer. In order to provide right answers, the system is connected with a knowledge-base (K-B), which contains facts. During the process of answering, the system queries the KB, retrieves a set of candidate facts and generates a correct answer to the question using the right fact. The generated answer may contain two types of "words": one is common words for composing the answer (referred to as common word) and the other is specialized words in the KB denoting the answer (referred to as KB-word).

To learn a GENQA model, we assume that each training instance consists of a question-answer pair with the KB-word specified in the answer. In this paper, we only consider the case of *simple factoid question*, which means each question-answer pair is associated with a single fact (i.e., one triple) of the KB. Without loss of generality, we mainly focus on forward relation QA, where the question is on *subject* and *predicate* and the answer points to *object*. Tables 1 shows some examples of the training instances.

Dataset: To facilitate research on the task of generative QA, we create a new dataset by collecting data from the web. We first build a knowledge-base by mining from three Chinese encyclopedia web sites[1]. Specifically we extract entities and associated triples (*subject, predicate, object*) from the structured parts (e.g. HTML tables) of the web pages. Then the extracted data is normalized and aggregated to form a knowledge-base. In this paper we sometimes refer to the items of a triple as a constituent of knowledge-base. Second, we collect question-answer pairs by extracting from two Chinese community QA sites[2].

Table 2: Statistics of the QA data and the knowledge-base.

Community QA	Knowledge-base	
#QA pairs	#entities	#triples
235,171,463	8,935,028	11,020,656

Table 2 shows the statistics of the knowledge-base and QA-pairs.

We construct the training and test data for GENQA by "grounding" the QA pairs with the triples in knowledge-base. Specifically, for each QA pair, a list of candidate triples with the *subject* fields appearing in the question, is retrieved by using the Aho-Corasick string searching algorithm. The triples in the candidate list are then judged by a series of rules for relevance to the QA pair. The basic requirement for relevance is that the answer contains the *object* of the triple, which specifies the KB-word in the answer. Besides, we use additional scoring and filtering rules, attempting to find out the triple that truly matches the QA pair, if there is any. As the result of processing, 720K instances (tuples of question, answer, triple) are finally obtained with an estimated 80% of instances being truly positive. The data are publicly available online[3].

In order to test the generalization ability of the GENQA model, the data is randomly partitioned into training dataset and test dataset by using triple as the partition key. In that way, all the questions in the test data are regarding to the unseen facts (triples) in the training data. Table 3 shows some statistics of the datasets. By comparing the numbers of triples in Table 2 and Table 3, we can see that a large portion of facts in the knowledge-base are not present in the training and test data, which demonstrates the necessity for the model to generalize to unseen facts.

1 Baidu Baike, Baike.com, Douban.com

2 Baidu Zhidao, Sogou Wenwen

3 `https://github.com/jxfeb/Generative_QA`

Table 3: Statistics of the training and test dataset for GENQA

Training Data		Test Data	
#QA pairs	#triples	#QA pairs	#triples
696,306	58,019	23,364	1,974

2 The Neural Model

Let $Q = (x_1, \ldots, x_{T_Q})$ and $Y = (y_1, \ldots, y_{T_Y})$ denote the natural language question and answer respectively. The knowledge-base is organized as a set of triples (*subject*, *predicate*, *object*), each denoted as $\tau = (\tau_s, \tau_p, \tau_o)$. Inspired by the work on the encoder-decoder framework for neural machine translation (Cho et al., 2014; Sutskever et al., 2014; Bahdanau et al., 2015) and neural natural language dialogue (Shang et al., 2015; Vinyals and Le, 2015; Serban et al., 2015), and the work on question answering with knowledge-base embedding (Bordes et al., 2014b; Bordes et al., 2014a; Bordes et al., 2015), we propose an end-to-end neural network model for GENQA, which is illustrated in Figure 1.

The GENQA model consists of **Interpreter**, **Enquirer**, **Answerer**, and an external knowledge-base. **Answerer** further consists of **Attention Model** and **Generator**. Basically, **Interpreter** transforms the natural language question Q into a representation $\mathbf{H}_Q$ and saves it in the short-term memory. **Enquirer** takes $\mathbf{H}_Q$ as input to interact with the knowledge-base in the long-term memory, retrieves relevant facts (triples) from the knowledge-base, and summarizes the result in a vector $\mathbf{r}_Q$. The **Answerer** feeds on the question representation $\mathbf{H}_Q$ (through the **Attention Model**) as well as the vector $\mathbf{r}_Q$ and generates the answer with **Generator**. We elaborate each component hereafter.

Interpreter: Given the question represented as word sequence $Q = (x_1, \ldots, x_{T_Q})$, Interpreter encodes it to the array of vector representations. In our implementation, we adopt a bi-directional RNN as in (Bahdanau et al., 2015), which processes the sequence in forward and reverse order by using two independent RNNs (here we use gated recurrent unit (GRU) (Chung et al., 2014)). By concatenating the hidden states (denoted as $(\mathbf{h}_1, \cdots, \mathbf{h}_{T_Q})$), the embeddings of the words (denoted as $(\mathbf{x}_1, \cdots, \mathbf{x}_{T_Q})$), and the original one-hot representations of the words, we obtain an array

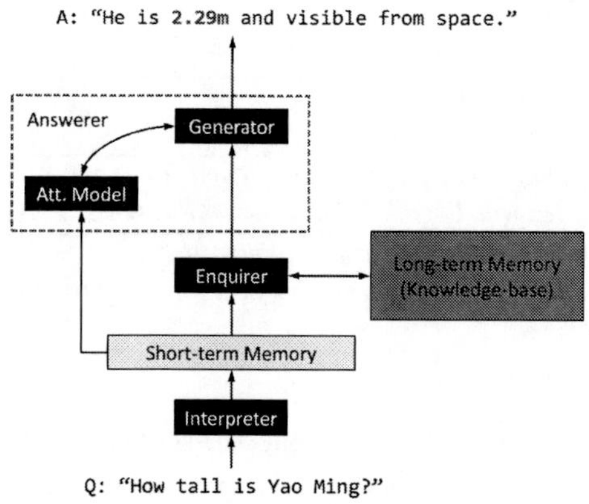

Figure 1: The diagram for GENQA.

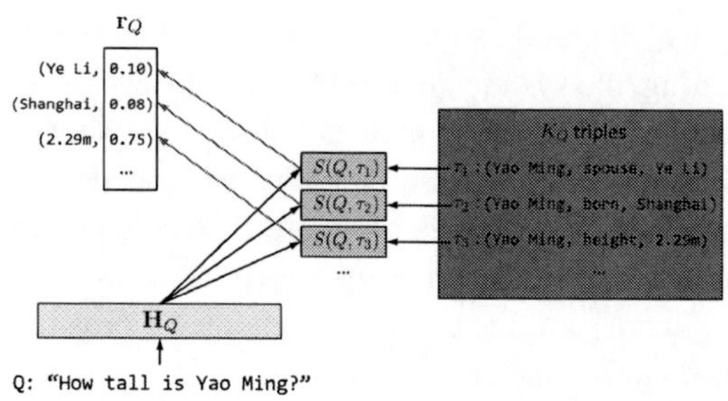

Figure 2: The Enquirer of GENQA.

of vectors $\mathbf{H}_Q = (\tilde{\mathbf{h}}_1, \cdots, \tilde{\mathbf{h}}_{T_Q})$, where $\tilde{\mathbf{h}}_t = [\mathbf{h}_t; \mathbf{x}_t; x_t]$. This array of vectors is saved in the short-term memory, allowing for further processing by Enquirer and Answerer for different purposes.

Enquirer: Enquirer "fetches" the relevant facts from the knowledge-base with Q and $\mathbf{H}_Q$ (as illustrated by Figure 2). Enquirer first performs term-level matching to retrieve a list of relevant candidate triples, denoted as $\mathcal{T}_Q = \{\tau_k\}_{k=1}^{K_Q}$. K_Q is the number of candidate triples, which is usually less than several hundreds in our data. This first round filtering, although fairly simple, is important in making the following step of differentiable operations (e.g., the weighting on the candidate set and the answer generation) and optimization feasible. After obtaining $\mathcal{T}_Q$, the task reduces to evaluating the relevance of each candidate triple with the question in the embedded space(Bordes et al., 2014b; Bordes et al., 2014a).

More specifically Enquirer calculates the matching scores between the question and the K_Q triples.

For question Q, the scores are represented in a K_Q-dimensional vector $\mathbf{r}_Q$ where the kth element of $\mathbf{r}_Q$ is defined as the probability

$$r_{Q_k} = \frac{e^{S(Q,\tau_k)}}{\sum_{k'=1}^{K_Q} e^{S(Q,\tau_{k'})}},$$

where $S(Q, \tau_k)$ denotes the matching score between question Q and triple τ_k.

The probability in $\mathbf{r}_Q$ will be further taken into the probabilistic model in Answerer for generating a particular answering sentence. Since $\mathbf{r}_Q$ is of modest size, after the filtering step, and differentiable with respect to its parameters, it can be effectively optimized by the supervision signal in recovering the original answers through back-propagation.

In this work, we provide two implementations for Enquirer to calculate the matching scores between question and triples.

Bilinear Model: The first implementation simply takes the average of the word embedding vectors in $\mathbf{H}_Q$ as the representation of the question (with the result denoted as $\bar{\mathbf{x}}_Q$) . For each triple τ in the knowledge-base, it takes the mean of the embeddings of its *subject* and *predicate* as the representation of the triple (denoted as $\mathbf{u}_\tau$). Then we define the matching score as

$$\bar{S}(Q,\tau) = \bar{\mathbf{x}}_Q^\top \mathbf{M} \mathbf{u}_\tau,$$

where $\mathbf{M}$ is the matrix parameterizing the matching between the question and the triple.

CNN-based Matching Model: The second implementation employs the convolutional neural network (CNN) for modeling the matching score between question and triple, as in (Hu et al., 2014) and (Shen et al., 2014). Specifically, the question is fed to a convolutional layer followed by a max-pooling layer, and summarized as a fixed-length vector, denoted as $\hat{\mathbf{h}}_Q$. Then $\hat{\mathbf{h}}_Q$ and $\mathbf{u}_\tau$ (again as the mean of the embedding of the corresponding *subject* and *predicate*) are concatenated as input to a multi-layer perceptron (MLP) to produce their matching score

$$\hat{S}(Q,\tau) = f_{\text{MLP}}([\hat{\mathbf{h}}_Q; \mathbf{u}_\tau]).$$

For this model the parameters consist of both the CNN for question representation and the MLP for the final matching decision.

Answerer: Answerer uses an RNN to generate the answer sentence based on the information of question saved in the short-term memory (represented by $\mathbf{H}_Q$) and the relevant knowledge retrieved from the long-term memory (indexed by $\mathbf{r}_Q$), as illustrated in Figure 3. The probability of generating the answer sentence $Y = (y_1, y_2, \ldots, y_{T_Y})$ is defined as

$$p(y_1, \cdots, y_{T_Y} | \mathbf{H}_Q, \mathbf{r}_Q; \theta) = p(y_1 | \mathbf{H}_Q, \mathbf{r}_Q; \theta) \prod_{t=2}^{T_Y} p(y_t | y_1, \ldots, y_{t-1}, \mathbf{H}_Q, \mathbf{r}_Q; \theta)$$

where θ represents the parameters in the GENQA model. The conditional probability in the RNN model (with hidden state $\mathbf{s}_1, \cdots, \mathbf{s}_{T_Y}$) is specified by $p(y_t|y_1, \ldots, y_{t-1}, \mathbf{H}_Q, \mathbf{r}_Q; \theta) = p(y_t|y_{t-1}, \mathbf{s}_t, \mathbf{H}_Q, \mathbf{r}_Q; \theta)$.

In generating the tth word y_t in the answer sentence, the probability is given by the following mixture model

$$\begin{aligned} p(y_t|y_{t-1}, \mathbf{s}_t, \mathbf{H}_Q, \mathbf{r}_Q; \theta) = \\ p(z_t = 0|\mathbf{s}_t; \theta) p(y_t|y_{t-1}, \mathbf{s}_t, \mathbf{H}_Q, z_t = 0; \theta) + \\ p(z_t = 1|\mathbf{s}_t; \theta) p(y_t|\mathbf{r}_Q, z_t = 1; \theta), \end{aligned}$$

which sums the contributions from the "language" part and the "knowledge" part, with the coefficient $p(z_t|\mathbf{s}_t; \theta)$ being realized by a logistic regression model with $\mathbf{s}_t$ as input. Here the latent variable z_t indicates whether the tth word is generated from a common vocabulary (for $z_t = 0$) or a KB vocabulary ($z_t = 1$). In this work, the KB vocabulary contains all the *objects* of the candidate triples associated with the particular question. For any word y that is *only* in the KB vocabulary, e.g., "`2.29m`", we have $p(y_t|y_{t-1}, \mathbf{s}_t, \mathbf{H}_Q, z_t = 0; \theta) = 0$, while for y that does not appear in KB, e.g., "`and`", we have $p(y_t|\mathbf{r}_Q, z_t = 1; \theta) = 0$. There are some words (e.g., "`Shanghai`") that appear in both common vocabulary and KB vocabulary, for which the probability contains nontrivial contributions of both bodies.

In generating common words, Answerer acts in the same way as the decoder RNN in (Bahdanau et al., 2015) with information from $\mathbf{H}_Q$ selected by the attention model. Specifically, the hidden state at t step is computed as $\mathbf{s}_t = f_s(y_{t-1}, \mathbf{s}_{t-1}, c_t)$ and $p(y_t|y_{t-1}, \mathbf{s}_t, \mathbf{H}_Q, z_t = 0; \theta) = f_y(y_{t-1}, \mathbf{s}_t, c_t)$,

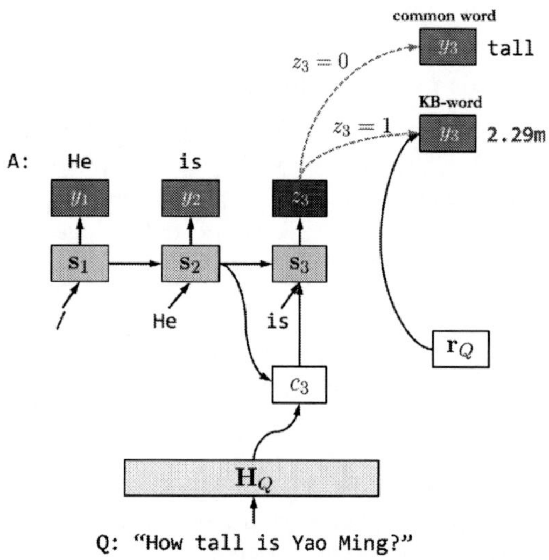

Figure 3: The Answerer of GENQA.

where c_t is the context vector computed as weighted sum of the hidden states stored in the short-term memory $\mathbf{H}_Q$.

In generating KB-words via $p(y_t|\mathbf{r}_Q, z_t = 1; \theta)$, Answerer simply employs the model $p(y_t = k|\mathbf{r}_Q, z_t = 1; \theta) = r_{Q_k}$. The better a triple matched with the question, the more likely the *object* of the triple is selected.

Training: The parameters to be learned include the weights in the RNNs for Interpreter and Answerer, parameters in Enquirer, and the word-embeddings which are shared by the Interpreter RNN and the knowledge-base. GENQA, although essentially containing a retrieval operation, can be trained in an end-to-end fashion by maximizing the likelihood of observed data, since the mixture form of probability in Answerer provides a unified way to generate words from common vocabulary and (dynamic) KB vocabulary. In practice the model is trained on machines with GPUs by using stochastic gradient-descent with mini-batch.

3 Experiments

3.1 Comparison Models

To our best knowledge there is no previous work on generative QA, we choose three baseline methods: a neural dialogue model, a retrieval-based QA model and the embedding based QA model, respectively corresponding to the generative aspect and the KB-retrieval aspect of GENQA:

Neural Responding Machine (NRM): NRM (Shang et al., 2015) is a neural network based generative model specially designed for short-text conversation. We train the NRM model on the question-answer pairs in the training data with the same vocabulary as the vocabulary of GENQA. Since NRM does not access the knowledge-base during training and test, it actually remembers all the knowledge from the QA pairs in the weights of the model.

Retrieval-based QA: the knowledge-base is indexed by an information retrieval system (we use Apache Solr), in which each triple is deemed as a document. At test phase, a question is used as the query and the top-retrieved triple is returned as the answer. Note that in general this method cannot generate natural language answers.

Embedding-based QA: as proposed by (Bordes et al., 2014a; Bordes et al., 2014b), the model is learnt from the question-triple pairs in the training data. The model learns to map questions and knowledge-base constituents into the same embedding space, where the similarities between questions and triples are computed as the inner product of the two embedding vectors.

Since we have two implementations of matching score in Enquirer of the GENQA model, we denote the one using the bilinear model as GENQA and the other using CNN and MLP as $\text{GENQA}_{\text{CNN}}$.

3.2 Results

We evaluate the performance of the models in terms of 1) accuracy, i.e., the ratio of correctly answered questions, and 2) the fluency of answers. In order to ensure an accurate evaluation, we randomly select 300 questions from the test set, and manually remove the nearly duplicate cases and filter out the mistaken cases (e.g., non-factoid questions).

Accuracy: Table 4 shows the accuracies of the models in the test set. NRM has the lowest accuracy, showing the lack of ability to remember the answers accurately and generalize to questions unseen in the training data. For example, to question "`Which country does Xavi play for as a midfielder?`" (Translated from Chinese), NRM gives the wrong answer "`He plays for France`" (Translated from Chinese), since the

Figure 4: Examples of the generated answers by GENQA.

ID	Questions	Generated Answers
1	三国演义谁写的? Who wrote the Romance of the Three Kingdoms?	明朝的罗贯中。 Luo Guanzhong in Ming dynasty.
2	项羽是哪国人? Which state does Xiang Yu belong to?	楚国的皇帝。 King of the Chu State.
3	还珠格格多少集? How many episodes does My Fair Princess have?	一共24集。 24 episodes in total.
4	泰戈尔是哪国作家? Which country is the writer Tagore from?	泰戈尔是印度著名的作家 。 Tagore is a famous Indian writer.
5	孙燕姿今年多大啊? How old is Stefanie Sun this year?	32岁，他出生于1978年7月23日。 Thirty-two, he was born on July 23, 1978.
6	《格列佛游记》的作者是谁? Who is the author of Gulliver's Travels?	法国作家斯威夫特。 The French writer, Swift.
7	怪物史莱克4什么时候上映呀? When will Shrek Forever After be released?	上映日期：梦工厂电影发行公司。 Release date: DreamWorks Pictures.
8	凤凰卫视是哪里的电视台? Which place is phoenix television located at?	总部在刘长乐。 The headquarters is at Liu Changle.

Table 4: Test accuracies

Models	Test
Retrieval-based QA	36%
NRM	19%
Embedding-based QA	45%
GENQA	47%
GENQA$_{\text{CNN}}$	**52%**

athlete actually plays for Spain. The retrieval-based method achieves a moderate accuracy, but like most string-matching methods it suffers from word mismatch between the question and the triples in KB. The embedding-based QA model achieves higher accuracy on test set, thanks to its generalization ability from distributed representations. GENQA and GENQA$_{\text{CNN}}$ are both better than the competitors, showing that GENQA can further benefit from the end-to-end training for sequence-to-sequence learning. For example, as we conjecture, the task of generating the appropriate answer may help the learning of word-embeddings of the question. Among the two GENQA variants, GENQA$_{\text{CNN}}$ achieves the best accuracy, getting over half of the questions right. An explanation for that is that the convolution layer helps to capture salient features in matching. The experiment results demonstrate the ability of GENQA models to find the right answer from KB even with regard to new facts. For example, to the example question mentioned above, GENQA gives the correct answer "He plays for Spain".

Fluency: We make some empirical comparisons and find no significant differences between NRM and GENQA in terms of the fluency of answers. In general, all the three models based on sequence generation yield correct patterns in most of the time.

3.3 Case Study

Figure 4 gives some examples of generated answers to the questions in the test set by our GENQA models, with the underlined words generated from KB. Clearly it can smoothly blend the KB-words and common words in the sentence, thanks to the unified neural model that can learn to determine the right time to place a KB-word or a common word. We notice that most of the generated answers are short sentences, for which there are two possible reasons: 1) many answers to the factoid questions on the Community QA sites are usually short, and 2) we select the answers by beam-searching the sequence with maximum log-likelihood normalized by its length, which generally prefers short answers. Examples 1 to 4 show the correctly generated answers, where the model not only matches the right triples (and thus generate the right KB-words), but also generates suitable common words surrounding them. However, in some cases like examples 5 and 6 even the right triples are found, the surrounding common words are improper or incorrect from the knowledge-base point of view (e.g., in example 6 the author "Jonathan Swift" is from Ireland rather than France). By investigating the correctly generated answers on test data, we find roughly 8% of them having improper surrounding words. In some other cases, the model fails to match the correct triples with the questions, which produces completely wrong answers. For the instance in example 7, the question is about the release date of a movie, while the model finds its distributor and generates an answer incorrect both in terms of fact and language.

References

[Bahdanau et al.2015] Dzmitry Bahdanau, Kyunghyun Cho, and Yoshua Bengio. 2015. Neural machine translation by jointly learning to align and translate. In *ICLR*.

[Bordes et al.2014a] Antoine Bordes, Jason Weston, and Sumit Chopra. 2014a. Question answering with subgraph embeddings. *EMNLP*.

[Bordes et al.2014b] Antoine Bordes, Jason Weston, and Nicolas Usunier. 2014b. Open question answering with weakly supervised embedding models. In *ECML PKDD*, pages 165–180.

[Bordes et al.2015] Antoine Bordes, Nicolas Usunier, Sumit Chopra, and Jason Weston. 2015. Large-scale simple question answering with memory networks. *arXiv preprint arXiv:1506.02075*.

[Cho et al.2014] Kyunghyun Cho, Bart Van Merriënboer, Caglar Gulcehre, Dzmitry Bahdanau, Fethi Bougares, Holger Schwenk, and Yoshua Bengio. 2014. Learning phrase representations using rnn encoder-decoder for statistical machine translation. *EMNLP*.

[Chung et al.2014] Junyoung Chung, Caglar Gulcehre, KyungHyun Cho, and Yoshua Bengio. 2014. Empirical evaluation of gated recurrent neural networks on sequence modeling. *arXiv preprint arXiv:1412.3555*.

[Hu et al.2014] Baotian Hu, Zhengdong Lu, Hang Li, and Qingcai Chen. 2014. Convolutional neural network architectures for matching natural language sentences. In *Advances in Neural Information Processing Systems*, pages 2042–2050.

[Serban et al.2015] Iulian V Serban, Alessandro Sordoni, Yoshua Bengio, Aaron Courville, and Joelle Pineau. 2015. Building end-to-end dialogue systems using generative hierarchical neural network models. *arXiv preprint arXiv:1507.04808*.

[Shang et al.2015] Lifeng Shang, Zhengdong Lu, and Hang Li. 2015. Neural responding machine for short-text conversation. In *Association for Computational Linguistics (ACL)*, pages 1577–1586.

[Shen et al.2014] Yelong Shen, Xiaodong He, Jianfeng Gao, Li Deng, and Grégoire Mesnil. 2014. Learning semantic representations using convolutional neural networks for web search. In *Proceedings of the companion publication of the 23rd international conference on World wide web companion*, pages 373–374. International World Wide Web Conferences Steering Committee.

[Sutskever et al.2014] Ilya Sutskever, Oriol Vinyals, and Quoc VV Le. 2014. Sequence to sequence learning with neural networks. In *NIPS*, pages 3104–3112.

[Vinyals and Le2015] Oriol Vinyals and Quoc Le. 2015. A neural conversational model. *arXiv preprint arXiv:1506.05869*.

[Weston et al.2015] Jason Weston, Sumit Chopra, and Antoine Bordes. 2015. Memory networks. In *International Conference on Learning Representations (ICLR)*.

"A Distorted Skull Lies in the Bottom Center..." Identifying Paintings from Text Descriptions

Anupam Guha,[1] Mohit Iyyer,[1] Jordan Boyd-Graber[2]
[1]University of Maryland, Department of Computer Science and UMIACS
[2]University of Colorado, Department of Computer Science
aguha@cs.umd.edu, miyyer@umiacs.umd.edu,
Jordan.Boyd.Graber@colorado.edu

Abstract

Most question answering systems use symbolic or text information. We present a dataset for a task that requires understanding descriptions of visual themes and their layout: identifying paintings from their descriptions. We annotate paintings with contour data, align regions with entity mentions from an ontology, and associate image regions with text spans from descriptions. A simple embedding-based method applied to text-to-image coreferences achieves state-of-the-art results on our task when paired with bipartite matching. The task is made all the more difficult by scarcity of training data.

1 Knowledge from Images

Question answering is a standard NLP task that typically requires gathering information from knowledge sources such as raw text, ontologies, and databases. Recently, vision and language have been amalgamated into an exciting and difficult task: using images to ask or answer questions.

While humans can easily answer complex questions using knowledge gleaned from images, visual question answering (VQA) is difficult for computers. Humans excel at this task because they abstract key concepts away from the minutiae of visual representations, but computers often fail to synthesise prior knowledge with confusing visual representations.

We present a new instance of visual question answering: can a computer identify an artistic work given only a textual description? Our dataset contains images of paintings, tapestries, and sculptures covering centuries of artistic movements from dozens of countries. Since these images are of cultural importance, we have access to many redundant descriptions of the same works, allowing us to create a naturalistic but inexpensive dataset. Due to the complex and oblique nature of questions about paintings, their visual complexity, and the relatively small data size, prior approaches used for VQA over natural images are infeasible for our task.

We formalise the task in Section 3, where we also present a preliminary system (ARTMATCH) and compare with it a data-driven text baseline to illustrate the usefulness and versatility of our method (Section 4). Finally, in Section 5 we compare our task and system to previous work that combines NLP and vision.

2 Describing Art

University Challenge (UK) or quiz bowl (USA) has previously been studied for question answering using text-based methods (Boyd-Graber et al., 2012). However, some quiz bowl questions are inherently visual in that their answers are works of art.

Figure 1 shows an example of a painting description and associated annotations (to be described later) from a quiz bowl question. Identifying paintings from textual descriptions of their contents is difficult; for example, many disparate paintings feature two men (*Stag at Sharky's*, *The Sacrifice of Isaac*, and *Kindred Spirits*). Given their varied style, composition, and depiction, how do we teach computers to infer the *meaning* of a painting?

To capture the meaning, we rely on redundant descriptions of entities in paintings offered by multiple text spans in these questions. The man on the right in Figure 1 is variously described as a "Frenchman", "a diplomat", "a man in black", and "George de Selve".

Proceedings of 2016 NAACL Human-Computer Question Answering Workshop, pages 43–47,
San Diego, California, June 12-17, 2016.

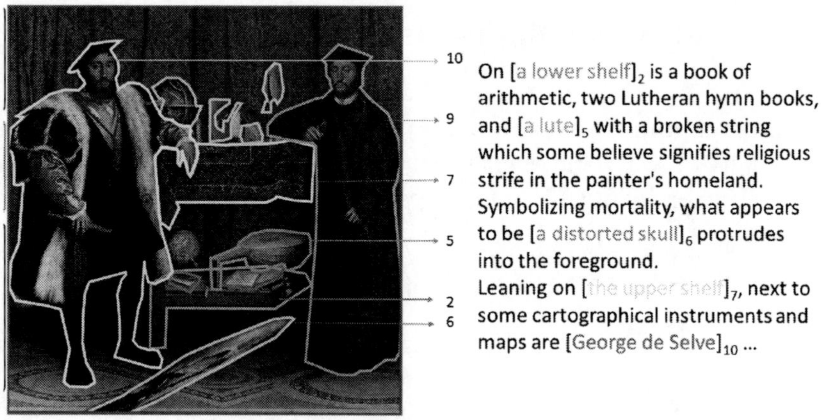

Figure 1: A painting (left) with image regions matched to coreference chains in a question (right). The question uses a variety of oblique mentions to make the trivia question more difficult; some entities (e.g., de Selve) are mentioned again later in the question.

We can use this redundancy to learn the meaning of the pixels within the red contour.

In text, this is the problem of coreference resolution (Radford, 2004) as the multiple text spans refer to the same "real world" entity. Trivia questions have complex descriptive coreferent groupings (Guha et al., 2015). Thus, to annotate our dataset we map coreference groups in question text to regions in paintings using LabelMe (Russell et al., 2008), providing a direct mapping of text spans to groups of pixels in the images and their spatial properties.

Our dataset contains 128 paintings,[1] where each painting is the answer to a single quiz bowl question. First, we assign each object in a painting to a single class from an ontology with eight coarse and fifty two fine (level two) classes. This ontology is three levels deep and follows the hyponymy structure of ImageNet (Deng et al., 2009).[2] Then, we map each coreference group from the question text to an image contour from the painting (see Table 1). As the questions come from a game, the mentions are often oblique, making them hard to answer with text alone. For instance, a description of *Rain, Steam, and Speed* will avoid explicitly mentioning the painting's central object by name (a "locomotive") in favor of describing it in a roundabout way (e.g., a "conveyance").

[1]Annotated data and code available after blind review.

[2]Ontology provided as supplementary material.

Number of ...	dataset
Unique Paintings	128
Objects with contours	1,436
Coreferring text groups	1,104
Object gross classes	8
Object fine classes	52

Table 1: Statistics of our new question answering dataset

3 Identifying Paintings from Text

Given one of the questions in our dataset, our goal is to provide the name of the painting that it describes. Because our focus is not on building better feature extractors for paintings, we assume that we have gold visual annotations (e.g., object contours, classes, and locations).[3] The task is challenging due to the size of our dataset (only 128 annotated question/painting pairs), which prevents the training of most machine learning models, as well as high visual complexity and vagueness in question text.

3.1 A Text-Only Baseline

Our baseline model is "blind" in that it does not use any visual features to solve the task. We use the deep averaging network (Iyyer et al., 2015, DAN),

[3]When applied to paintings, state-of-the-art semantic segmentation models (Zheng et al., 2015) trained on natural images are only reliable for four coarse object classes (vs 60 coarse and fine ones), which leads to near-random accuracies for ARTMATCH.

which takes as input a textual description of a painting and learns a 128-label classifier over an average of embeddings from words in the question. Since this model does not do any visual mapping, we collect unannotated questions about our 128 paintings to form a respectably-sized training set of 503 questions. While the DAN has access to more data than our non-blind model, we hope that we can improve over the baseline using visual information.

3.2 Answer Questions Using Annotated Paintings

Our method, which we call ARTMATCH, assumes that some of the groups of coreferent text in a question describe visual objects in the associated painting. If we have a unified vector representation of visual object classes from painting regions and textual coreferent groups, a bipartite mapping can match them.

3.2.1 Matching Mentions to Images

To identify the painting described by a question, we first convert every question to a list of objects obtained from coreference chains (e.g., *a lute*, *a distorted skull*). On the painting side, we have a list of annotated visual objects. These two lists form the nodes of a bipartite graph on which we perform a maximum cardinality match (Hopcroft and Karp, 1973), where edge weights represent match strength. We consider the painting with the most matched edges as the answer; in case of a tie, the painting with the highest cumulative edge weight wins.

This process requires that our visual object classes are in the same vector space as objects found in textual coreference chains. For one chain, we compute a vector representation by averaging the embeddings of its words.[4] Also, for each visual object class, we obtain a set of synonyms and hyponyms and compute an averaged word vector over this set. Similarly, we produce averaged vectors over location and number attributes (e.g., the *single* attribute is represented by a vector average over $\{$*single, one, a, an*$\}$). Since distance between word embeddings measures semantic similarity, we assign an object class and attributes that have the highest cosine similarity to that chain's vector representation, as shown in Figure 2.

[4]We use publicly available 300-dimensional word2vec embeddings trained on Google News (Mikolov et al., 2013).

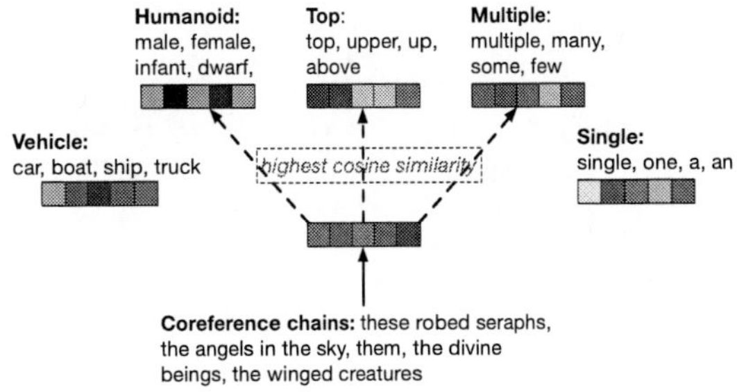

Figure 2: Using word2vec representations from coreferent groupings in a description to deduce object class and attributes by cosine similarity.

We easily combine ARTMATCH's matching with DAN by modifying the weight of a bipartite match by multiplying that weight with the probability of that question-answer pair being correct as given by DAN.

4 Performance and Analysis

We investigate the performance both locally (matching specific objects) and globally (identifying the correct image) before doing an error analysis.

First, we examine the **individual matching on objects** and measure accuracy on three different tasks:

1. Does ARTMATCH properly match coarse and fine visual *object classes* to question text (e.g., is "an angel" mentioned in the question matched to an image region depicting an angel)?[5]
2. Are the matches is in the correct *locations* (e.g., is the "angel" in the top-left corner?)?
3. Is the *number* of objects correctly matched (e.g., are there two or three angels)?

Table 2 shows the results of these experiments. Additionally, for the highest-scoring paintings (the answers output by ARTMATCH), 13.2% of objects are exactly matched with location and number; without considering those attributes, 20.4% of fine-grained classes are matched.

Next, we look at the main task of **identifying the correct painting**. As Table 3 shows, ARTMATCH nearly matches the blind DAN baseline with just the coarse and fine object classes. Spatial location and number attributes boost ARTMATCH above the baseline, and combining both systems pushes accuracy

[5]Coarse class metrics are provided for all objects while fine class performance is only for those that have fine annotations.

Feature	P	R	F1
Coarse object class	0.72	0.38	0.45
Fine object class	0.72	0.60	0.60
Object location	0.32	0.25	0.24
Object number	0.96	0.81	0.88

Table 2: Individual metrics of classes and features detected by word embeddings from coreference chains describing objects

Method	accuracy
DAN	59.4%
ARTMATCH: fine objects	42.0%
ARTMATCH: all objects	58.6%
ARTMATCH: objects+attributes	61.7%
ARTMATCH+DAN	**65.7%**

Table 3: Our system vs the blind baseline. DAN is trained on 503 questions but has no visual information. ARTMATCH has visual features from paintings but no training data. Combining both leads to a significant increase in performance.

by four absolute points, indicating that the models are learning complementary information.

Having established that our simple method of incorporating visual information can achieve significant gains in accuracy, we now proceed to analyse instances in which our system does well and the DAN does not (and vice-versa).

4.1 Error Analysis

There are 34 questions for which the DAN fails but ARTMATCH succeeds. For many of these questions, the DAN fails because it overfits to common clues. Given a test question about *Melencholia I*, the DAN answers *Madonna with the Long Neck*, as the training questions about both paintings repeatedly mention a female figure and cherubs. However, the question also mentions geometric figures, the spatial locations of which enable ARTMATCH to answer correctly.

Conversely, there are thirty-one questions where ARTMATCH fails but DAN succeeds. Some of these questions contain text constructs such as the painter's name that are repeated in both training and test questions, which makes it easy for the DAN to solve (e.g., "Identify this most famous work of Claude Monet"). In other cases, ARTMATCH answers incorrectly because of spurious matches due to substantial visual similarity between various objects in paintings. For example, in a question about *The Holy Trinity* by Masaccio, "St. John" is assigned the close but incorrect class of "statue" while "Jesus" is correctly identified as a person. Further confused with spatial similarities between the paintings, ARTMATCH's answer is *Supper at Emmaus*, which has Jesus but no St. John. In other cases, peripheral similarity leads to the central mismatch being overlooked, motivating an an attention mechanism to focus on "significant" entities for future work (Mnih et al., 2014).

5 Related Work

Our work is specifically related to previous work on visual question answering and more generally to multimodal applications of vision and language.

Visual QA has previously focused on content questions (Antol et al., 2015; Ren et al., 2015; Andreas et al., 2015), while we focus on identity questions. Relatedly, Zhu et al. (2015) find semantic links between images and text via an attention model.

We use coreference to connect text and image regions, similar to Kong et al. (2014). However, not all text is "visual" (Dodge et al., 2012) and not all image regions can be described textually (Berg et al., 2012). While we focus on meaning, structure of text (Elsner et al., 2014) can also be inferred from images. Socher et al. (2014) match sentences to images; however, our dataset is unique in that the text is intentionally oblique (rather than direct descriptions) and our images—paintings—are more varied visually.

Aside from QA, images have been successfully used to generate captions (Karpathy and Fei-Fei, 2014; Mao et al., 2014; Vinyals et al., 2014; Xu et al., 2015; Chen and Zitnick, 2014). While we use vision to aid an NLP task, others have gone in the opposite direction, inducing correspondences between words and video clips (Yu and Siskind, 2013), words and action models (Ramanathan et al., 2013), and language and perception (Matuszek et al., 2012).

6 Conclusion and Future Work

The major contribution of this work is to extend question answering to a complex visual setting by presenting an annotated dataset and a simple system that manages to exceed the performance of a strong text-only baseline QA system. The next challenge is to scale up this dataset to enable end-to-end training pipelines for answering questions using raw images.

References

Jacob Andreas, Marcus Rohrbach, Trevor Darrell, and Dan Klein. 2015. Deep compositional question answering with neural module networks. *arXiv preprint arXiv:1511.02799*.

Stanislaw Antol, Aishwarya Agrawal, Jiasen Lu, Margaret Mitchell, Dhruv Batra, C. Lawrence Zitnick, and Devi Parikh. 2015. Vqa: Visual question answering. In *International Conference on Computer Vision*.

Alexander C Berg, Tamara L Berg, Hal Daume III, Jesse Dodge, Amit Goyal, Xufeng Han, Alyssa Mensch, Margaret Mitchell, Aneesh Sood, Karl Stratos, et al. 2012. Understanding and predicting importance in images. In *Computer Vision and Pattern Recognition*.

Jordan Boyd-Graber, Brianna Satinoff, He He, and Hal Daumé III. 2012. Besting the quiz master: Crowdsourcing incremental classification games. In *Empirical Methods in Natural Language Processing*.

Xinlei Chen and C Lawrence Zitnick. 2014. Learning a recurrent visual representation for image caption generation. *arXiv preprint arXiv:1411.5654*.

Jia Deng, Wei Dong, Richard Socher, Jia Li, Kai Li, and Li Fei-Fei. 2009. ImageNet: A Large-Scale Hierarchical Image Database. In *Computer Vision and Pattern Recognition*.

Jesse Dodge, Amit Goyal, Xufeng Han, Alyssa Mensch, Margaret Mitchell, Karl Stratos, Kota Yamaguchi, Yejin Choi, Hal Daumé III, Alexander C Berg, et al. 2012. Detecting visual text. In *Proceedings of the Association for Computational Linguistics*.

Micha Elsner, Hannah Rohde, and Alasdair DF Clarke. 2014. Information structure prediction for visual-world referring expressions. *Proceedings of the European Chapter of the Association for Computational Linguistics*.

Anupam Guha, Mohit Iyyer, Danny Bouman, and Jordan Boyd-Graber. 2015. Removing the training wheels: A coreference dataset that entertains humans and challenges computers. In *North American Association for Computational Linguistics*.

John E Hopcroft and Richard M Karp. 1973. An n^5/2 algorithm for maximum matchings in bipartite graphs. *SIAM Journal on computing*, 2(4):225–231.

Mohit Iyyer, Varun Manjunatha, Jordan Boyd-Graber, and Hal Daumé III. 2015. Deep unordered composition rivals syntactic methods for text classification. In *Association for Computational Linguistics*.

Andrej Karpathy and Li Fei-Fei. 2014. Deep visual-semantic alignments for generating image descriptions. *arXiv preprint arXiv:1412.2306*.

Chen Kong, Dahua Lin, Mayank Bansal, Raquel Urtasun, and Sanja Fidler. 2014. What are you talking about? text-to-image coreference. In *Computer Vision and Pattern Recognition*.

Junhua Mao, Wei Xu, Yi Yang, Jiang Wang, and Alan L Yuille. 2014. Explain images with multimodal recurrent neural networks. *arXiv preprint arXiv:1410.1090*.

Cynthia Matuszek, Nicholas FitzGerald, Luke Zettlemoyer, Liefeng Bo, and Dieter Fox. 2012. A joint model of language and perception for grounded attribute learning. *arXiv preprint arXiv:1206.6423*.

Tomas Mikolov, Kai Chen, Greg Corrado, and Jeffrey Dean. 2013. Efficient estimation of word representations in vector space. *arXiv preprint arXiv:1301.3781*.

Volodymyr Mnih, Nicolas Heess, Alex Graves, et al. 2014. Recurrent models of visual attention. In *Proceedings of Advances in Neural Information Processing Systems*.

Andrew Radford. 2004. *English syntax: An introduction*. Cambridge University Press.

Vignesh Ramanathan, Percy Liang, and Li Fei-Fei. 2013. Video event understanding using natural language descriptions. In *International Conference on Computer Vision*.

Mengye Ren, Ryan Kiros, and Richard Zemel. 2015. Exploring models and data for image question answering. In *Proceedings of Advances in Neural Information Processing Systems*.

Bryan C Russell, Antonio Torralba, Kevin P Murphy, and William T Freeman. 2008. Labelme: a database and web-based tool for image annotation. *International Journal of Computer Vision*.

Richard Socher, Andrej Karpathy, Quoc V Le, Christopher D Manning, and Andrew Y Ng. 2014. Grounded compositional semantics for finding and describing images with sentences. *Transactions of the Association for Computational Linguistics*.

Oriol Vinyals, Alexander Toshev, Samy Bengio, and Dumitru Erhan. 2014. Show and tell: A neural image caption generator. *arXiv preprint arXiv:1411.4555*.

Kelvin Xu, Jimmy Ba, Ryan Kiros, Aaron Courville, Ruslan Salakhutdinov, Richard Zemel, and Yoshua Bengio. 2015. Show, attend and tell: Neural image caption generation with visual attention. *arXiv preprint arXiv:1502.03044*.

Haonan Yu and Jeffrey Mark Siskind. 2013. Grounded language learning from video described with sentences. In *Proceedings of the Association for Computational Linguistics*.

Shuai Zheng, Sadeep Jayasumana, Bernardino Romera-Paredes, Vibhav Vineet, Zhizhong Su, Dalong Du, Chang Huang, and Philip Torr. 2015. Conditional random fields as recurrent neural networks. In *International Conference on Computer Vision*.

Yuke Zhu, Oliver Groth, Michael Bernstein, and Li Fei-Fei. 2015. Visual7w: Grounded question answering in images. *arXiv preprint arXiv:1511.03416*.

Using Confusion Graphs to Understand Classifier Error

Davis Yoshida and **Jordan Boyd-Graber**
davis.yoshida@colorado.edu, jordan.boyd.graber@colorado.edu

Abstract

Understanding the nature of the errors of a machine learning system is often difficult for multiclass classification problems with a large number of classes. This is true even more so if the number of examples for each class is low. To interpret the performance of a multiclass classifier, we form a graph representing the errors, and use average-link clustering to find groups of classes which are confused with each other. We apply this idea to the QANTA question answering system (Iyyer et al., 2014), and provide a method of analysis of the clusters.

1 Introduction

A typical development process for a machine learning pipeline involves many iterations of error analysis, and changes to each step of the pipeline. One of the most common tools for understanding the errors of multiclass classifiers is a confusion matrix. If, however, the number of classes is very large relative to the number of samples, the confusion matrix will be both large and sparse. This is problematic for error analysis, because adding a feature which reduces the confusion between two classes amounts to decreasing the overall error by a tiny increment. If the error is attacked on a class by class basis, the process will be both very lengthy and result in features which may not discriminate between any pairs of classes other than the one they were created for. While it is certainly possible to engineer features which are widely useful, it would be beneficial to do so this both consistently and quickly.

One example of a multiclass classification system with a large number of classes is QANTA, a factoid question answering system. QANTA is designed to play the Quiz Bowl trivia game, in which players are given questions word by word, and want to answer the question correctly as early as possible. Since the number of answers QANTA is trained on is finite, it can be viewed as a multiclass classifier with a large number of classes. For any given pair of answers, it is highly unlikely that there are more than a few questions for which the system confused one answer with the other. This makes QANTA a perfect example of a multiclass classifier which has a sparse confusion matrix. To better analyze the errors committed by the system we form a confusion graph for each of three subsets of our data. The construction of these graphs and some of their interesting properties are discussed in Section 2.

In Section 3, we discuss the use of average-link agglomerative clustering to find clusters of answers which are highly confused with each other on a validation set.

In Section 4, we apply the Autoslog system (Riloff, 1996) to each cluster to find find textual features which occur frequently in each cluster.

2 The Confusion Graph

After training QANTA, we use the errors it commits on a validation set to form the confusion graph. In this graph, the vertices are answers (classes), and the undirected weighted edges represent errors. Specifically, an edge (u, v) with weight w means that the fraction of questions having u as their correct answer while the system predicted v, or vice versa, is w.

Proceedings of 2016 NAACL Human-Computer Question Answering Workshop, pages 48–52,
San Diego, California, June 12-17, 2016.

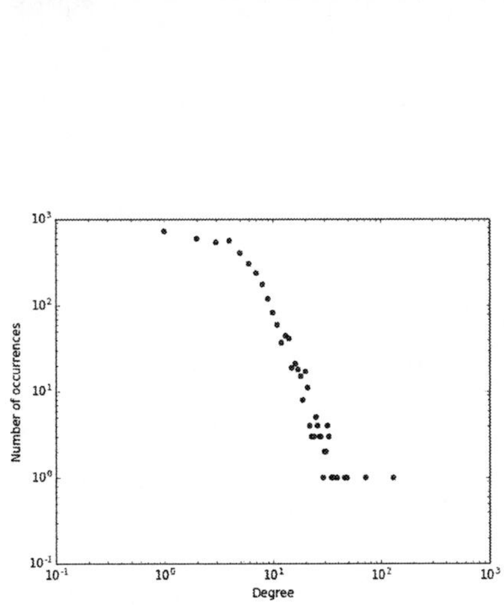

(a) Degree distribution for main validation set

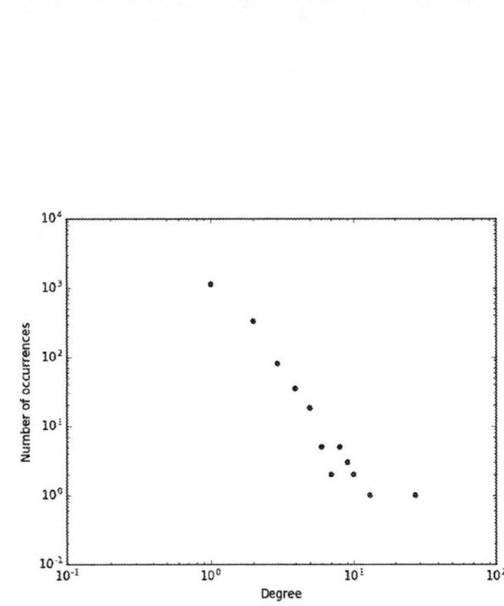

(b) Degree distribution for secondary validation set

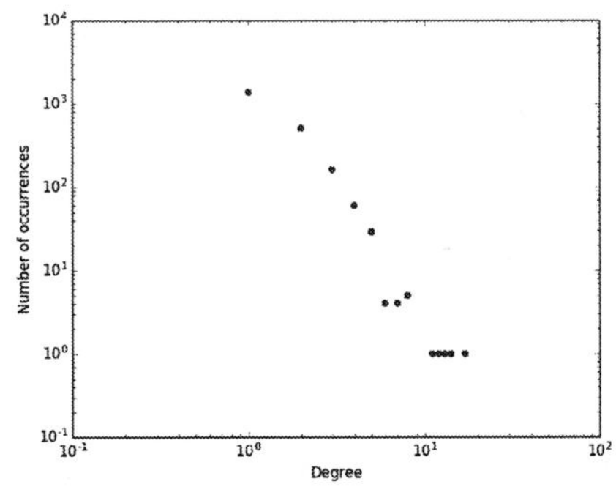

(c) Degree distribution for test set

Figure 1: Degree Distributions for confusion graphs. In these graphs the vertices are classes and the edges are misclassifications made by QANTA.

In order to simplify computation, the graph includes only answers that were confused with at least one other, as the rest would just be isolated vertices. We built these graphs for two of our validation sets, and our test set. The question/answer data that comprises these sets is unfortunately proprietary, so we cannot show examples of question/answer pairs here. Refer to the paper (Iyyer et al., 2014) for an example.

2.1 The Giant Component

Recall that our goal is to form groups of answers that are highly confused with each other. An optimistic plan would be to simply find the components of the graph, and split each one into a pair of clusters. Unfortunately, it turns out that QANTA's confusion graph for the primary validation set has very few components. Specifically, 4032 of the 4091 nodes in the graph are in a single, large component.

The reason for the emergence of a giant component is that there are certain answers (vertices) that have extremely high degrees, i.e. the degree distribution of these graphs is heavy-tailed. The degree distributions of each graph are shown in Figure 1. The existence of these high degree nodes leads to connectivity between seemingly very different answers.

For example, in the validation set, the most confused answer was the play: *Angels in America: A Gay Fantasia on National Themes.* It was confused with 131 different answers ranging from the number eight, to Milk, to ASCII. This shows that the errors made on this validation set did not solely include answers that are very similar.

2.2 Diameter and Neighborhoods

We now examine some of the other properties of the giant component of this graph. The diameter (i.e. maximum length of a shortest path between two vertices) of the component is 14. This means that every answer can be reached from every other, along a relatively short path. As an example, one of the few answer with an eccentricity of 14 is "Ribosome". It

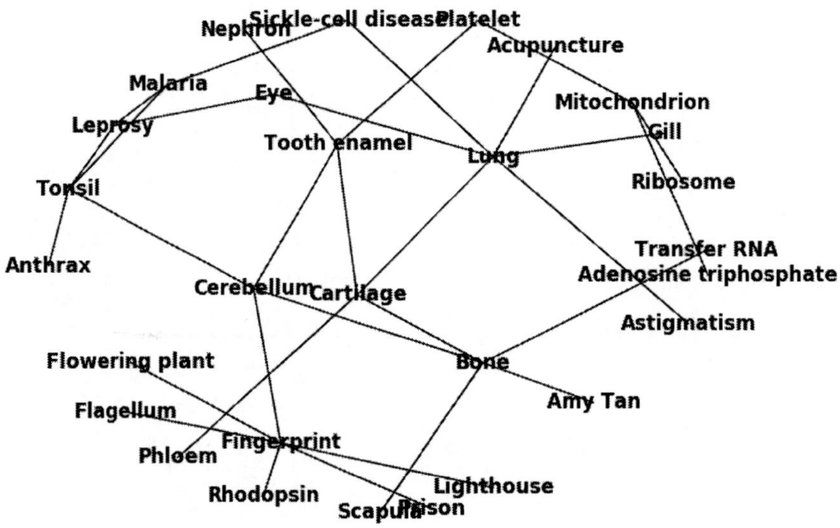

Figure 2: Answers within a short distance of the answer "Ribosome" where edges represent QANTA answering one when the other should be answered.

is a distance of 14 away from the novel *Ragtime*, via the path:
Ribosome → Mitochondrion → Platelet → Tooth enamel → Cartilage → Lung → Acupuncture → Yoga → Caste system in India → Jacques Cartier → HMS Beagle → Thor Heyerdahl → Ragtime → Ragtime (novel).

So at least one question that should have been answered Ribosome was answered as Mitochondrion (or vice versa), the same for Mitochondrion and Platelet, and so on. This is a very characteristic example of the paths connecting examples. Typically, most of the errors are between related answers, but there will be some jump which switches the topic abruptly. Here, the first few answers in the path are biology related, Acupuncture is used as a medical treatment, and yoga comes from India. The connections Caste System in India → Jacques Cartier and Thor Heyerdahl → Ragtime, however, are not expected.

A subgraph of the confusion graph, consisting of all nodes within a distance of 6 from Ribosome is shown in Figure 2. Aside from for some exceptions at maximal distance (e.g. Lighthouse and Amy Tan), all of the nodes are biology related.

The neighborhood of the answer Bessel Function is shown in Figure 3. Note that here is an overlap with the previous neighborhood via the node Astigmatism. In this neighborhood we see a small bunch of computing and mathematical terms, as well as some whose presences again escape an immediate explanation (e.g. Bhagavad Gita).

This exploration hints that although the graph is essentially one component there are clusters of related answers which are confused with each other

3 Clustering Classes

We would like to find clusters of related answers, as in the previous section, but in an algorithmic way. To this end, we run average linkage agglomerative clustering (Murtagh, 1983) on the graph, using the weights defined in the previous section.

Average-link clustering on a confusion graph proceeds by first initializing a singleton cluster for each class. Then, at each step, the two clusters, C_i, C_j are selected such that they have largest average weight

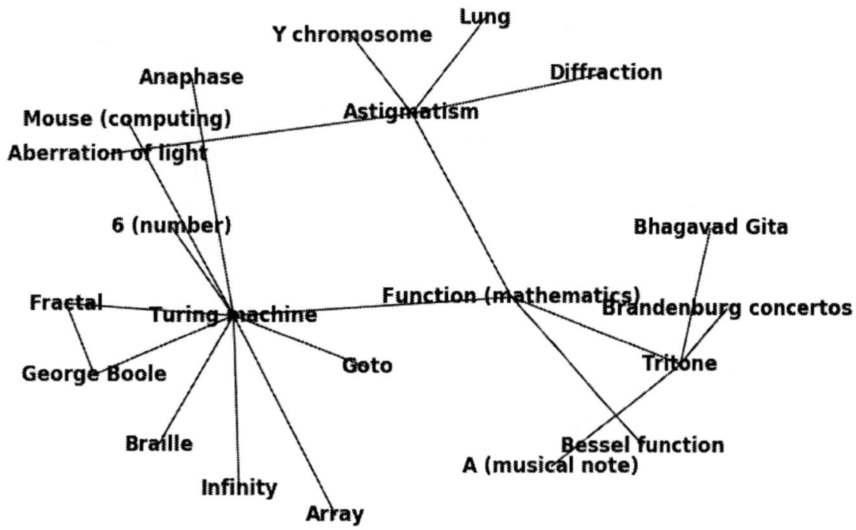

Figure 3: Answers within a short distance of the answer "Ribosome" where edges represent QANTA answering one when the other should be answered.

between them, i.e.:

$$i, j = \underset{i,j}{\operatorname{argmax}} \frac{1}{|C_i||C_j|} \sum_{u \in C_i} \sum_{v \in C_j} w(u, v)$$

where $w(u, v)$ is the weight of the edge (u, v) if it exists, or 0 otherwise. These clusters are then merged into a single cluster, and the process is repeated until all nodes are in a single cluster. There are 4091 nodes in the graph, so there will be 4090 joining steps. Average-linkage clustering is $O(N^2 \log(N))$, so this computation will become difficult for much larger class sets.

In the context of a confusion graph, two clusters being merged indicates that the classes in the clusters are highly confused. In order to understand our errors better, we examine these clusters. It turns out that many of them are a single answer being added to a larger cluster. To filter out these, we only look at pairs of at least a minimum size, s and having a maximum difference of d, i.e. C_i and C_j such that $\min(|C_i|, |C_j|) \geq s$ and $||C_i| - |C_j|| \leq d$.

When $s = 8$ and $d = 1$, we found 46 pairs of clusters. Examples are shown in Tables 1 and 2. Cluster 1 of Table 1 seems highly related to high energy physics and cosmology, whereas Cluster 2, while similar looks related to a different branch of physics with a dash of chemistry. Cluster 1 of Table 2 has many quantities (e.g. energy and enthalpy), with a few other technical terms thrown in. Cluster 2 has a few units and technical terms, but also Leibniz, who is understandably related to science. Unlike the previous cluster pair, there are also some totally unrelated classes: the author Kingsley Amis and his novel *Lucky Jim*, and the novel *The Ox-Bow Incident*.

Some clusters fail to be remotely interpretable, but a large number are of similar quality to the ones shown here: Largely related, with a few outliers thrown in. These clusters give us a tractable way of interpreting the confusion of our classifier.

4 Cluster Analysis with Autoslog

Autoslog is a system which find repeated patterns of parts of speech in a corpus of documents. An example of such a pattern is "Battle of ¡Noun phrase¿". For each cluster developed in the previous section,

Cluster 1	Cluster 2
Theory of Relativity	Pauli Exclusion Principle
Time Dilation	Alloy
Reynolds Number	Electronegativity
Cosmological Constant	Bessemer Process
Sunspot	Nuclear Fission
Muon	Hydrogen Peroxide
Speed of Light	Fraunhofer lines
Kinetic Energy	Palladium
Dark Energy	Platinum
	Hund's Rules

Table 1

Cluster 1	Cluster 2
Quicksort	Tachyon
Hyperbola	Monad
Work (physics)	Time
Fault (geology)	Kingsley Amis
Energy	The Ox-Bow Incident (Novel)
Variance	Gravitational Constant
Frequency	Lucky Jim
Median	Mass
Standard Deviation	Gottfried Wilhelm Leibniz
Enthalpy	Kilogram
Circle	Ossian
Scattering	

Table 2

Clusters of answers which QANTA confuses with each other often.

we use the set of questions mapping to an answer in the cluster as a corpus, and run Autoslog on it. We then filter to patterns which occur much more frequently in that correspond to one set of questions but not the other.

For example, in Cluster 1 of Table 1, the pattern "[Verb phrase: be] [Adjective Phrase: equal]" was found. It matches any verb phrase with the root verb of "to be" followed by an adjective phrase with the root of "equal". This pattern should match statements about the various constants and quantities found in the cluster.

For another pair of clusters in which one is composed mostly of nations and locations, and the other is mostly chemicals, we find the patterns "[Noun phrase: capital] of" and "[Noun phrase: Nation] with". However, the pattern "[Verb phrase: Named] for" occurs about equally as much in each cluster. Such patterns may be part of what contributes to the classifier confusing the clusters.

5 Future Work

We have developed and examined confusion graphs for our classifier, but not yet applied them to improving its performance. We would like to add the patterns found by Autoslog as features for QANTA, and evaluate its increase in performance. If this is successful, we can again build a confusion graph, find patterns and add them as features, and repeat the process. This is a sort of automatic feature engineering. How much performance improvement we can get out of this method is an open question.

6 Conclusion

Confusion graphs can help us understand the nature of the errors occurring in a classifier when the number of classes is very large. We have applied this to examine the errors of the question answering system, QANTA. From the graph, we derive clusters of answers which are easily confused, and find textual features which discriminate between the clusters.

References

Mohit Iyyer, Jordan Boyd-Graber, Leonardo Claudino, Richard Socher, and Hal Daumé III. 2014. A neural network for factoid question answering over paragraphs. In *Empirical Methods in Natural Language Processing*.

Fionn Murtagh. 1983. A survey of recent advances in hierarchical clustering algorithms. *The Computer Journal*, 26(4):354–359.

Ellen Riloff. 1996. Automatically generating extraction patterns from untagged text. In *Proceedings of the national conference on artificial intelligence*, pages 1044–1049. AAAI Press.

Paraphrase for Open Question Answering: New Dataset and Methods

Ying Xu[†], **Pascual Martínez-Gómez**[‡],
Yusuke Miyao[§], **Randy Goebel**[†]
[†]Department of Computing Science, University of Alberta
[‡]National Institute of Advanced Industrial Science and Technology (AIST)
[§]National Institute of Informatics / JST, PRESTO
[†]{yx2, rgoebel}@ualberta.ca
[‡]pascual.mg@aist.go.jp
[§]yusuke@nii.ac.jp

Abstract

We propose a new open question answering framework for question answering over a knowledge base (KB). Our system uses both a curated KB, Freebase, and one that is extracted automatically by an open information extraction model, IE KB. Our system consists of only one layer of paraphrase, compared to the three layers used in a previous open question answering system (Fader et al., 2014). However, because of the more accurately extracted relation triples in IE KB, combined with linked entities from IE KB to Freebase, our system achieves a 7% absolute gain in F_1 score over the previous system.

1 introduction

There are two broad classes of systems that provide question answering (QA) from a knowledge base (KB). One uses semantic parsing (Berant and Liang, 2014; Reddy et al., 2014; Yih et al., 2015), and the other uses information extraction (IE). Semantic parsing systems depend on highly accurate knowledge bases such as Freebase, which are accurate but incomplete (Riedel et al., 2013; Fader et al., 2014). However, although semantic parsing systems currently achieve higher performance than IE-based systems, we think it is desirable to continue to develop the latter as an alternative or in combination with the former.

One major challenge for question answering from a KB is the many ways in which relations can be expressed. On the one hand, we need to deal with language variability, for example, acknowledging that the following two questions have the same meaning: "*What character did Natalie Portman play in Star Wars?*" and "*What is the role of Natalie Portman in Star Wars?*". We call this NL-NL paraphrasing, since it requires the identification of a map between two natural language expressions. On the other hand, we need to bridge the gap between the expression of relations in a curated knowledge base, such as Freebase, and relations conveyed in natural language sentences. We refer to this as NL-KB paraphrasing. For instance, general QA will require a mapping between the natural language relation *brother* and the Freebase relation "/people/person/sibling_s."

Our contribution to Open IE question answering is three-fold. First, we provide a new wide-coverage store of automatically extracted relation triples, which has a higher precision than that of previous work (Fader et al., 2014). This Open IE triple store allows us to tackle the NL-NL paraphrasing problem. Second, the entities in our dataset is linked to Freebase, which allows us to tackle the NL-KB paraphrasing problem. Third, we propose a simple and effective open QA framework that consists of a single paraphrase layer. In this framework, we perform searches on both Open IE KB and Freebase. This single-layered paraphrase model allows us to test and compare a variety of paraphrasing models. Experiments on the WebQuestion set (Berant et al., 2013) shows that our system exhibits better performance than the two IE-based systems (Fader et al. (2014), Yao and Van Durme (2014)), and is comparable to (Berant et al., 2013), where their average F-score is 35.7%, and ours is 37.9%.

Proceedings of 2016 NAACL Human-Computer Question Answering Workshop, pages 53–61,
San Diego, California, June 12-17, 2016.

2 Related Work

A current major research thread in QA is to cast it as a semantic parsing problem, where the objective is to map a natural language question into a formal language, i.e., a database query. This query is then run on a database, and results are returned to the user.

SCISSOR (Ge and Mooney, 2005) was one of the first successful attempts to create a robust semantic parser. It worked by first syntactically parsing a question, augmenting the result with semantic information, and then transforming the result into a logical language. However, this process requires a large volume of training supervision, namely "gold standard" annotations of semantically-augmented syntactic trees paired with their logical representations. Its demonstration was limited to GeoQuery (Zelle and Mooney, 1996), which is a very restricted domain and database. A more recent approach to achieve robust, open-domain semantic parsing is that of Berant et al. (2013), where the training supervision is limited to pairs of questions and answers. In their approach, they use latent λ-DCS (Liang, 2013) logical formulas for their meaning representations, which can be converted deterministically into Sparql queries on Freebase. Yih et al. (2015) developed the best performing semantic parser on the WebQuestion set (Yih et al., 2015). Inspired by (Yao and Van Durme, 2014), instead of searching on the whole knowledge base, they defined a query graph which is more closely related to the target entity in the questions.

Regarding IE QA systems, there are two representatives. Yao and Van Durme (2014) constructs a graph structure to represent each KB topic, which is searched to retrieve answers to questions. Fader et al. (2014)'s system constructs the KB as a triple database, where each triple consists of two entities and one relation phrase. In the base of the KB approach, we follow the design of the latter, by querying on the relation triple database. Moreover, our knowledge base contains both curated data, i.e., Freebase, and our own automatically extracted IE KB. Our relation triples were also extracted from the ClueWeb09 corpus, but we used the Open IE system of Xu et al. (2015), which is based on dependency parsing. There are two main differences between our triples and Fader's: 1. we achieve higher precision of triple extraction, partly because of the dependency parser; 2. our entities are linked to Freebase by an entity linking approach, instead of pure string match. These two differences provide both higher precision and higher recall for question answering.

Fader et al. (2014)'s system exploits several levels of paraphrase. One is the process of paraphrasing from one question to another question, for example, from "How does _ affect your body?" to "What body system does _ affect ?" One is *parsing*, which converts natural language questions into a small number of high-precision templates. For example, from "Who/What is NP_{arg}" to (arg, is-a, ?x). Another is query-rewriting, which is similar to our paraphrase operator. For example, its paraphrase operator re-writes *children* to *was born to*. Our system, however, only uses a single layer paraphrasing, which makes our approach simpler and more intuitive, while achieving higher performance.

3 Our DataSet

To augment our QA system, we create a new Open IE relation triple dataset that contains sentences and document IDs from which the triples are extracted. The relation triples are extracted from ClueWeb09 by the Open IE system of Xu et al. (2015). Each triple contains two arguments, which are entities from Freebase, and one relation phrase. The arguments' Freebase IDs are provided by FACC1 corpus[1]. The relations are lemmatized and the sentences that contain the triples are provided. As a result, the dataset contains more than 300 million relation triples[2].

Table 1 shows one relation triple example, including the originating parsed sentence. The relation triple is from the 485_{th} sentence of the document *clueweb12-0700tw-51-00204*. The relation word is *director*, which is the 4th word in the sentence. The two arguments *Raul Gonzalez* and *National Council of La Raza* have corresponding Freebase IDs: /m/02rmsx3 and /m/085f3n.

Many NLP tasks can potentially benefit from such data. For example, for question answering task, there are at least three advantages. One is that the

[1]http://lemurproject.org/clueweb09/

[2]We use only half of the ClueWeb09 because of resource limits.

Relation Triple Example
<doc>clueweb12-0700tw-51-00204 <relation>485, Raul Gonzalez /m/02rmsx3, National Council of La Raza /m/085f3n, <E1> →(appos) director →(prep_at) <E2> director 4 (ROOT (S (NP (NP (NNP Raul) (NNP Gonzalez)) (, ,) (NP (NP (JJ legislative) (NN director)) (PP (IN at) (NP (NP (DT the) (NNP National) (NNP Council)) (PP (IN of)(NP (NP (NNP La) (NNP Raza)) ...)

Table 1: Example of a relation triple extracted from ClueWeb09, with its source sentence and document ID.

entities are linked to Freebase, which will identify entities that represent one object but with different instances. Secondly, the triple is associated with the parsed sentences and the document ID, which can provide better evidence for questions with n-ary relations, such as "What character did Natalie Portman play in Star Wars?" Finally, we can provide explanations, i.e., by identifying sentences that are evidence in support of our answers. We believe that this large volume of linked triples may not only improve the mapping between the natural language and Freebase relations, but also improve the recall of questions, as we can also search based on entities' Freebase IDs. We intend to make this data publicly available.

4 System Structure

Figure 1 presents our general framework for open question answering.

The first component of our system is *query preprocessing*. We use the Stanford CoreNLP tool for entity extraction and sentence parsing. Entities such as persons and organizations have higher priority as target entities than those such as numbers and dates. We then extract the dependency path between the chosen target entity and the question phrase. The question phrase can be a single word such as *where* or multi-word phrases such as *which character*. The words on the dependency path are considered to be the relation words, i.e., the predicates.

The second component is our *paraphrase recognition*, i.e., the identification of a mapping between relations in the questions and relations in the two knowledge bases. Further details of our paraphrase models are in Section 5.

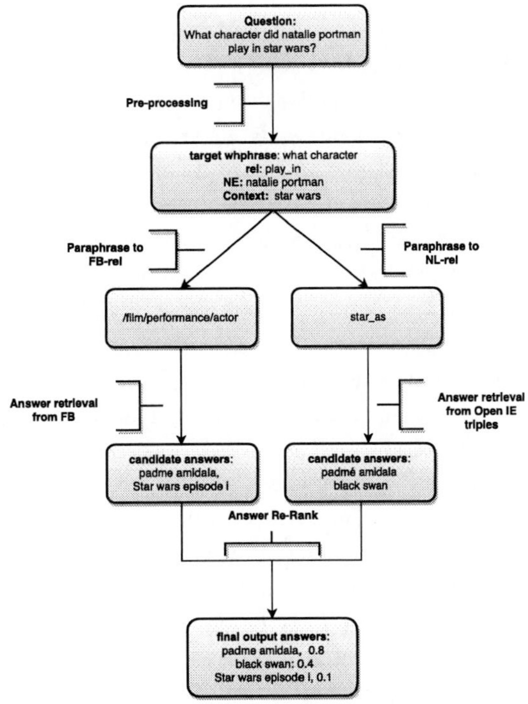

Figure 1: Our open question answering system structure.

The third component is *answer retrieval*. Our knowledge base contains triples from Open IE extraction and Freebase. We retrieve answers based on the target entity, the relation words in the question, the corresponding paraphrase relations, and context words.

The final component is *answer re-ranking*. Since we expect the system to retrieve multiple possible answers, those answers are re-ranked with an SVM-Rank system (Tsochantaridis et al., 2004). Further details of the model and its features are described in Section 7.

5 Paraphrase

Here we concentrate on word/phrase level paraphrase instead of sentence level paraphrase. We noticed that literal paraphrase may not be sufficient for accurate question answering. For example, that a person *lives* in a location, might not be a good paraphrase for a person *is buried* at a location. But the two have such high correlation that identifying the correlation will help answering questions such as "Where did a person live." The question answering community has currently chosen to adapt either a machine translation model or a simple pointwise mutual information (PMI) model. Here we present the three models we adapted for our question answering system.

The first one is a frequency based model. Paraphrase rules are learned based on the question answering training set. Given a set of questions, the relation words in the questions are extracted as mentioned in Section 4. Then we retrieve the relation triples in the KB that contain both the target entities and the answers. The score of a rule, query_Rel → KB_Rel, is the frequency of the entity pairs that the query relation and KB relation share.

The second is a PMI based model, which is adapted by (Fader et al., 2014)'s QA system. The general function of the PMI is:

$$log\frac{P(x,y)}{P(x)P(y)} \tag{1}$$

where $P(x) = count(x)/n$, n is the number of triples. For paraphrase, the frequency of unigrams represents the number of entity pairs associated with one relation. The frequency of bigrams represents the number of entity pairs shared by two relations.

The third is the highly-cited DIRT algorithm (Lin and Pantel, 2001). In this model, relations are represented by two vectors. Each vector represents one argument slot. Their similarity score function is defined as follows:

$$\sqrt{sim(v_l^x, v_l^y) * sim(v_r^x, v_r^y)}. \tag{2}$$

where v_l^x is a word vector representing the relation x's left argument slot. The value of the vectors is the PMI between the relation and the argument.

Our paraphrase model uses a subset of our highly accurate Open IE triples. The restriction is that the relation words should appear between the parsing dependency path of two entities, and that the maximum path length is 3. This restriction will increase the precision of the triples, and improve the performance of the paraphrase.

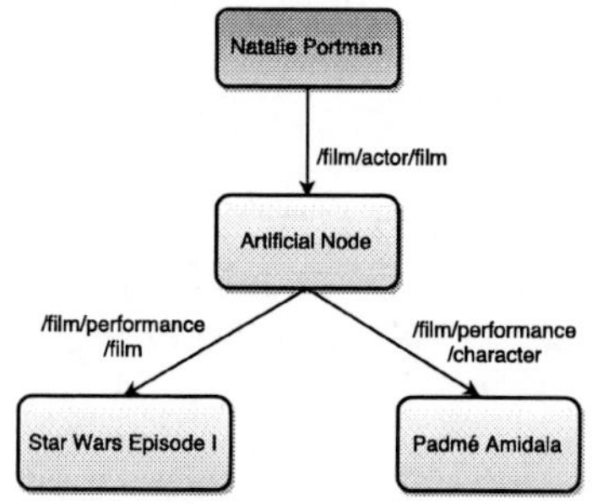

Figure 2: An example of compound artificial nodes.

6 Answer Retrieval

We designed our system so that we can search by both entity names and entity freebase IDs. In addition, the system also considers other context words of a question besides the target entity and relation words.

Our knowledge base contains triples from Open IE extractions and Freebase. The Open IE triples are extracted from ClueWeb documents using the models of (Xu et al., 2015). The Freebase triples contain entity pairs that are directly linked by a relation or by a compound relation, e.g., "/film/actor/film /film/performance/character," (Figure 2) which we hereafter abbreviate as "/film /character." Compound relations are represented by links that connect two entities with distance two. The middle node in between is an artificial node, instead of an entity. It is used to represent relations or events with multiple attributes, such as date, location etc. As pointed out by (Yao and Van Durme, 2014) compound relations are important for the question answering task.

We use Lucene, an information retrieval framework tool, to store the triples. Every triple is constructed as one document that contains 6 fields: left and right argument's surface forms, left and right argument's Freebase IDs, the relation phrase, and the context. The OpenIE triples' context are the sentences containing that triple. The Freebase triples' context are the compound node text for compound relations. For instance, the context of the triple (natalie portman, /film /character, padmé amidala) is "padmé amidala - Star Wars episode ii: attack of the clones - freebase data team - film performance."

To search for the answers, we identify the target named entity of the query and its Freebase IDs. The Freebase ID candidates are extracted by Freebase

API. We also identify the relation word set, which includes both the relations in the question and their paraphrases, as mentioned in Section 5. The original relations are assigned a weight of 2, while others are assigned with a normalized paraphrase score between $[0, 1]$. The normalization assigns 1 to the best paraphrase relations and 0 to the n_{th}, where n is the maximum number of paraphrases.

For explanation purposes, consider again the question "What character did Natalie Portman play in Star Wars?" We extract the top three Freebase ID candidates for *natalie portman*: {/m/0913p, /m/0dncctc, /m/05ngby1}. With the relation *play*, we build a relation set {*play*} ∪ {*/actor, /written_by, /character*} ∪ {*voice, set, quarterback, star, lead*}. The terms {*/actor, /written_by, /character*} are Freebase relations that have a high paraphrase score with *play*. The context is the word set of the sentence. We then search for the target entity on either the left argument slot or the right, the relation, and the context. The score of a retrieved triple is the weight of the hit relation's paraphrase score. Different relations can lead to the same answer; we currently sum the scores of all retrieved triples for one answer.

7 Supervised Re-Ranking

Answers retrieved by the previous step are based only on word match. Because of the noise retained in paraphrase and relation extraction, we need to add more information to filter incorrect answers. Here we incorporate some extra information as features of an SVM-Rank model (Tsochantaridis et al., 2004).

Table 2 shows the features we proposed for the re-ranking system. Freebase types are extracted according the candidate answer's Freebase IDs, and the value of the Freebase relation /type. As there are thousands of types in Freebase, we further focus by reducing the types to around 100 clusters, as proposed by (Ling and Weld, 2012). The type feature will consider the types of answers, and diminishes those retrieved answers with an inconsistent type. Another source of type information is taken from our Open IE triples. We observe that most types can be considered as a relation between entities. For example, in the triple (Shakespeare, a playwright, England) *Playwright* is a relation between *Shakespeare* and *England*, and can be considered as one type of *Shakespeare*. This leads to our Feature 4: for example, for the question "which country invades Poland" with the candidate answer *Germany*, the feature is the frequency of (*country, Germany*) in the Open IE triple set.

For extra information from the paraphrase rules, we use the rule itself and the scores, which can be determined from the three different paraphrase models.

The *context words hit rate* feature is determined by the percentage of context words in the question that are also in the triple's context words. The target entity, the relation words and question words are excluded from context words. This can improve the answering of questions with n-ary relations. For example, for the question *What character did Natalie Portman play in Star Wars?* we check how many words in the set {Star, Wars} are in the candidate answer's triple context. Suppose the two candidate answers are: *padmé amidala*, with context "padmé amidala - Star Wars episode ii: attack of the clones - freebase data team - film performance;" *black swan*, with context "academy award for actress in a leading role - 83rd academy awards - black swan - role: nina sayers - 2010 - nanette - award honor." The first answer's *context words hit rate* is 1, as the context has {Star, Wars}. The second has hit rate 0.

In training, we use the top n answers from both the Open IE and Freebase. However if a correct answer is ranked below n, we still add it as a training instance. This increases the number of positive training instances. In testing, we only re-rank the top n answers, where n is set according to the performance in the development set.

To combine Freebase and the Open IE KB, we have considered two alternatives. One combines the two sets of answers and then re-ranks the combined answer set. The other is to re-rank the two sets independently, and combine them by assigning weights to different KBs.

8 Experiments

We evaluate our question answering system based on the question set provided by Berant et al. (2013). The questions are generated by the Google Suggest API. The answers are created by Amazon Mechanical Turk. One property of this dataset is that the

Features ID	Feature description
1	Namespace: whether the answer is extracted from Open IE KB, Freebase KB, or both.
2	Candidate answer Freebase types + whphrase, e.g. /location/country + what country
3	Candidate answer Freebase types + relation in the question, e.g. /location/country + invade
4	Frequency of (the type word in the question, answer) in the ClueWeb
5	Shape of the answer (*e.g.* has numbers, multiwords) + the question phrase
6	Paraphrase rules
7	Whether the paraphrase rule from the 3000 training sentences
8	Paraphrase rule with the max score, its score, and which paraphrase approach leads to it
9	Context words hit rate
10	Score of the answer with answer retrieval

Table 2: Features for the Supervised System.

answers are guaranteed to be found in Freebase.

Our experiments attempt to answer several questions:

- Is our dataset useful for the paraphrase tasks?
- Which popular paraphrase approach is more suitable for question answering?
- Is our system better than other Information Extraction-based systems?

There are at least two metrics used in the literature:

1. Top 1 F_1 score, as used by (Fader et al., 2014). Every system outputs only one answer. The system's answer is the entity with highest score (randomly pick one if there is a tie). No answer is produced if the highest score is below a certain threshold. An answer is considered correct if the entity in the system's answer appears in the gold answer. The precision, recall and F_1 score are calculated globally:

$$\text{Precision} = \frac{\text{\# questions with correct answers}}{\text{\# questions with answers}}$$
$$\text{Recall} = \frac{\text{\# questions with correct answers}}{\text{\# questions}}$$

2. Average F_1 score (accuracy). This is used by semantic parsing question answering systems such as (Berant and Liang, 2014; Yih et al., 2015). For every question, the precision, recall and F_1 score are computed between the systems' answer set and the gold answer set. Then, the F_1 scores are averaged across all questions in the test set. This metric is used to reward partially-complete system answers.

In the following experiments, we will compare our system with Fader's with respect to the first metric, and the rest with the second metric.

8.1 The Effect of Dataset size

We demonstrate the effect of different dataset sizes by estimating a paraphrase PMI model from a smaller subset of our data, and then comparing QA systems' performance with these alternative paraphrase sets. Initially, we use the recall as the comparative metric. Recall is calculated as the percentage of questions that can be answered by the top 30 candidate answers retrieved. To filter the effect of features and supervised models, results are based on answer retrieval on Freebase, and no re-ranking is given.

For every question we extract the top 100 Freebase relations as paraphrase of one question relation (100 is set on a development set). The paraphrase score is used as weight on the answer retrieval phase. We use a PMI model as the paraphrase model metric.

Our baseline consists of 800k triples, which is larger than the size of one existing relation triple dataset from Riedel et al. (2013) (200k). The whole paraphrase set has 26 million triples. Note that this is a smaller number of triples but with higher precision, compared with the whole Open IE knowledge base (300 million). When using 800k triples, the recall is 10.7%, whereas we obtain a recall of 34.5% when using 26 million triples. We notice that the performance difference is dramatic.

8.2 Paraphrase

Here we show the paraphrase effect on the Freebase-based and IE KB based question answering systems.

As mentioned, for the paraphrase between question relations and Freebase relations, we extract the top 100 Freebase relations for one question relation.

models	recall on the top 30
Freq3000	63.2%
Freq3000+PMI	64.5%

Table 3: Comparing different paraphrase models. Recall on the top 30, based on Freebase.

models	recall on the top 40
Freq3000	40.5%
Freq3000 + PMI	40.8%
Freq3000 + DIRT	40.7%

Table 4: Comparing different paraphrase models. Recall on the top 40, based on Open IE KB.

The paraphrase score is used as a weight on the answer retrieval.

Table 3 shows the recall measure on the top 30 answers with alternative paraphrase models based on Freebase. Freq3000 is the case where we use only the 3000 training sentences and the Open IE triple set. Freq3000+PMI is the supervised paraphrase, Freq3000, plus the unsupervised paraphrase with the PMI measure. The results show that the unsupervised paraphrase, which maps between Open IE triples and FB triples, does improve recall. It is not meaningful to use DIRT here because the frequency of every triple is 1 in Freebase, and the frequency of (named entity 1, Freebase relation) is based on the number of values of this slot.

For the paraphrase between question relations and Open IE KB relations, we extract the top 10 Open IE relations for one question relation (6-10 do not display much difference on the development set). Table 4 shows the top 40 answer recall values, with alternative paraphrase models based on Open IE knowledge base. There is no obvious difference among the alternatives. The paraphrase between natural language relations is more difficult than paraphrase between natural language relations and Freebase relations. One reason might be that Open IE relation extraction noise is amplified within the overall process.

8.3 State-of-the-Art

As mentioned previously, our system is an Information Extraction (IE) based system. Table 5 shows the results of our system comparing with the other two IE based systems. Yao14 (Yao and Van Durme, 2014)'s system use FB knowledge base solely; while Fader14 (Fader et al., 2014) use both FB KB and Open IE KB. Our one layer system based on Freebase is much better than the one based on the IE triples. This makes the normal combination method failed, i.e. the two methods mentioned in Section 7. Instead, for the combination system we use OneLayer_IE 's results only when OneLayer_FB returns no answers. Our system is better than both the previous IE-based systems. It is better than Fader14 with an absolute F1 gain of 7% although both systems use FB KB and IE KB. Our system based solely on FB KB is already better than Yao14, which also is based on FB KB only. Notice instead of measured manually (as in Fader14), our system is automatically measured on the WebQuestion answer set, which means the performance is under-estimated, as we will show in Section 8.4.

We also compare our system with several semantic parsing-based systems: Berant *et al.* 's systems Berant13, Berant14; and Microsoft system MS15 (Yih et al., 2015), which is a semantic parsing-based system that achieves the current best performance on the WebQuestion set. Table 6 shows the results. Our system is the first information extraction based system that performs better than Berant13 on the Freebase data.

models	avg P	avg R	avg F_1
OneLayer_IE	29.0	24.2	20.4
Berant13	48.0	41.3	35.7
OneLayer_FB	48.3	45.0	37.2
OneLayer_combine	40.3	45.7	37.9
Berant14	40.5	46.6	39.9
MS15(FB search API)	49.8	55.7	48.4

Table 6: Results that compare our system with semantic parsing-based question answering systems.

8.4 Error Analysis

One problem of using the WebQuestion set as evaluation data is that the gold standard set is incomplete. This is caused both by incompleteness of Freebase and by human error. To show the effect of incompleteness on the test result, we annotated 400 development set questions, to determine whether the top answers from our systems are correct. Table 7 compares the results on the original answer set and the

models	top1_P	top1_R	top1_F_1	avg P	avg R	avg F_1
Fader14	-	-	35	-	-	-
Yao14(FB search API)	-	-	-	51.7	45.8	33.0
OneLayer_FB	44.7	39.5	**41.9**	48.3	45.0	37.2
OneLayer_IE	28.5	26.6	27.5	29.0	24.2	20.4
OneLayer_combine	41.4	40.3	40.8	40.3	45.7	**37.9**

Table 5: Results that compare our system with other IE-based question answering systems.

expanded answer set. With the top1 measure, the absolute difference is 10%. To avoid the manual annotation for every system, our future work will expand the answers for all the questions. We will also do a more complete analysis of the effect of the incomplete answer set on the training process.

dataset	top1_P	top1_R	top1_F_1
original	30.9	29.2	30.0
expanded	42.0	39.7	40.8

Table 7: The results of the open question answering system on the original development set and the one with expanded answers.

When we look more closely at our systems' errors, we notice that one problem of IE KB-based systems is that they can not find numbers or common nouns such as "writer" as an answer. This is because of a weakness in the data extraction process, which is designed to extract relations between named entities that are identified by the entity linking systems. Consider these two examples:

Question1 "what kinda music does john mayer sing?"
Gold standard "Rock music".
Our answer "your body is a wonderland", a song by john mayer.

Question2 "what does jennifer lopez do?"
Gold standard "Actor"
Our answer "american idol", a TV show where jennifer lopez was a judge.

This naturally creates a thread for future work: expand the Open IE triple set to include arguments with common nouns or numbers.

9 Conclusion

We have designed and tested a new open question answering (Open QA) framework for question answering over a knowledge base (KB). Our system consists of only one layer of paraphrase, compared to the three layers used in a previous open question answering system (Fader et al., 2014). However, because of the more accurately extracted relation triples, and use of linked entities from IE KB to Freebase, our system achieves a 7% absolute gain in F_1 score over the previous Open QA system.

An acknowledged problem with our data is that both arguments are named entities, which make our Open IE KB based-system unable to answer questions with answers that are common nouns or numbers. That will be addressed in future work.

References

Jonathan Berant and Percy Liang. 2014. Semantic parsing via paraphrasing. In *Association for Computational Linguistics (ACL)*.

Jonathan Berant, Andrew Chou, Roy Frostig, and Percy Liang. 2013. Semantic parsing on freebase from question-answer pairs. In *Proceedings of EMNLP*.

Anthony Fader, Luke Zettlemoyer, and Oren Etzioni. 2014. Open question answering over curated and extracted knowledge bases. In *Proceedings of the 20th ACM SIGKDD International Conference on Knowledge Discovery and Data Mining*, KDD '14, pages 1156–1165, New York, NY, USA. ACM.

Ruifang Ge and Raymond J. Mooney. 2005. A statistical semantic parser that integrates syntax and semantics. In *Proceedings of the Ninth Conference on Computational Natural Language Learning*, CONLL '05, pages 9–16, Stroudsburg, PA, USA. Association for Computational Linguistics.

Percy Liang. 2013. Lambda dependency-based compositional semantics. *CoRR*, abs/1309.4408.

Dekang Lin and Patrick Pantel. 2001. DIRT @SBT@discovery of inference rules from text. In

Proceedings of the Seventh ACM SIGKDD International Conference on Knowledge Discovery and Data Mining, KDD '01, pages 323–328, New York, NY, USA. ACM.

Xiao Ling and Daniel S. Weld. 2012. Fine-grained entity recognition. In *In Proc. of the 26th AAAI Conference on Artificial Intelligence*.

Siva Reddy, Mirella Lapata, and Mark Steedman. 2014. Large-scale semantic parsing without question-answer pairs. *Transactions of the Association for Computational Linguistics*, 2:377–392.

Sebastian Riedel, Limin Yao, Benjamin M. Marlin, and Andrew McCallum. 2013. Relation extraction with matrix factorization and universal schemas. In *Joint Human Language Technology Conference/Annual Meeting of the North American Chapter of the Association for Computational Linguistics (HLT-NAACL '13)*, June.

Ioannis Tsochantaridis, Thomas Hofmann, Thorsten Joachims, and Yasemin Altun. 2004. Support vector machine learning for interdependent and structured output spaces. In *Proceedings of the Twenty-first International Conference on Machine Learning*, ICML '04, pages 104–, New York, NY, USA. ACM.

Ying Xu, Christoph Ringlstetter, Mi-Young Kim, Randy Goebel, Grzegorz Kondrak, and Yusuke Miyao. 2015. A lexicalized tree kernel for open information extraction. In *Proceedings of the 2015 Conference of the Association for Computational Linguistics (ACL)*. Association for Computational Linguistics, July.

Xuchen Yao and Benjamin Van Durme. 2014. Information extraction over structured data: Question answering with freebase. In *Proceedings of the 52nd Annual Meeting of the Association for Computational Linguistics (Volume 1: Long Papers)*, pages 956–966. Association for Computational Linguistics.

Wen-tau Yih, Ming-Wei Chang, Xiaodong He, and Jianfeng Gao. 2015. Semantic parsing via staged query graph generation: Question answering with knowledge base. In *Proceedings of the Joint Conference of the 53rd Annual Meeting of the ACL and the 7th International Joint Conference on Natural Language Processing of the AFNLP*. ACL Association for Computational Linguistics, July.

John M. Zelle and Raymond J. Mooney. 1996. Learning to parse database queries using inductive logic programming. In *Proceedings of the Association for the Advancement of Artificial Intelligence*, pages 1050–1055.

Association for Computational Linguistics
209 N. Eighth Street
Stroudsburg, Pennsylvania 18360

ISBN 978-1-5108-2529-1

9 781510 825291

CURRAN ASSOCIATES INC.
proceedings.com